GAME CHANGERS: INSPIRATIONAL SPORTS STORIES

AN EMPOWERING PLAYBOOK FOR TEENS TO BUILD RESILIENCE, CRUSH GOALS AND CULTIVATE EXCEPTIONAL CHARACTER

DAN GOLD

*For my beautiful children, my family, all my loyal, loving friends
and my Dad, who taught me how to throw a ball and be a man*

CONTENTS

PRE-GAME

WINTER, 1980. A scrappy team of U.S. college hockey players faced the seemingly unbeatable Soviet Union in the Olympic semifinals. The Soviets, four-time defending gold medalists, had crushed Team USA 10-3 in an exhibition just weeks earlier. Against a backdrop of Cold War tensions, the odds seemed insurmountable, the outcome all but certain—or so the world thought. But on that frigid night in Lake Placid, something extraordinary happened. Goalie Jim Craig made save after remarkable save, Mark Johnson's buzzer-beater tied the game at the end of the first period and Mike Eruzione's iconic goal put the U.S. ahead in the third. The Soviets pressed relentlessly, but the Americans held firm until the final horn. Against all odds, the "Miracle on Ice" became a defining moment—not just of sport, but of grit, belief and the triumph of thinking big.

This is the power of sports: the ability to reveal the extraordinary potential within ordinary people and to teach lessons that extend far beyond the game. Sports can mirror many of life's challenges—how to develop self-confidence, how to face obstacles, how to adapt, how to rise under pressure and how to pursue something bigger than yourself. These are the lessons that form the foundation of *Game Changers: Inspirational Sports Stories*.

This book is more than a collection of entertaining sports tales; it is a guide to understanding the values and skills that make a difference in life. Within these pages, you'll meet athletes from all walks of life who have faced adversity, made bold choices and emerged stronger for it. You'll learn about resilience through setbacks, the courage it takes to lead, the patience required to persevere and the strength found in collaboration. These lessons are not confined to the playing field—they are the building blocks for navigating relationships, academics and future careers.

What sets this book apart is its unique approach to storytelling. Each chapter explores the journeys of multiple athletes, presented in pairs—often from diverse sports, time periods or backgrounds—all connected by a common theme. By comparing their struggles and triumphs, you'll gain a richer understanding of the lessons they offer. These paired narratives allow you to see challenges from multiple perspectives and explore how different paths can lead to similar truths.

Including some athletes with controversial or checkered pasts serves an important purpose: it reminds us that even celebrated figures are flawed and fallible. Their stories highlight themes of accountability, redemption and growth and explore the nuances of the human condition—success is rarely linear and human beings are complex and multilayered. They illuminate the ambiguities in achievement and emphasize transparency, integrity and the value of making amends, offering readers powerful lessons for their own lives.

At this moment in your life, as you're discovering who you are and shaping your future, the lessons from these stories are especially meaningful. They will help you see the value of persistence, the importance of self-reflection and the power of purpose. This book invites you to connect the stories you read to your own experiences, encouraging you to think deeply about the person you want to become.

Each of the eight chapters centers around a key theme, combining vivid storytelling with thought-provoking analysis. Reflective questions and activities at the end of each chapter help reinforce the lessons, turning ideas into actionable insights. Whether it's learning how to handle failure or understanding the dynamics of leadership, this book equips you with tools to face life's challenges with confidence and clarity.

Above all, *Game Changers* aims to inspire and empower. By stepping into the shoes of these athletes, you'll see how ordinary individuals achieve extraordinary things—not because they never stumble but because they learn to get back up. Their stories will show you how to find your own inner strength, stay true to your values and rise to meet whatever challenges life throws your way.

So, as you turn the pages, get ready to embark on an incredible journey. These stories aren't just about victories or defeats—they're about the human spirit, the lessons we carry and the paths we forge. Let's dive into the world of sports together and discover the timeless wisdom waiting within these pages. Game on!

1 SELF-DISCOVERY AND CONFIDENCE BUILDING

WHEN LIONEL MESSI was just 11 years old, he faced a challenge that could have ended his dreams before they even began. Diagnosed with a growth hormone deficiency, he needed daily injections to grow properly, a treatment his family struggled to afford. Almost 6,000 miles away, Serena Williams was swinging a tennis racket on the cracked courts of Compton, California. Her father, Richard, had big dreams for Serena and her sister Venus, despite the odds stacked against them in a sport dominated by those who didn't look like them. These two young athletes, from opposite corners of the globe, faced challenges that would have made many give up. But they didn't. Instead, they found their inner strength and their stories are powerful lessons in self-discovery and confidence that can inspire us all.

FINDING YOUR INNER ATHLETE: THE JOURNEY OF SERENA WILLIAMS AND LIONEL MESSI

Serena Williams' journey to tennis greatness began on the weathered asphalt courts of Compton, where the struggles of her neighborhood sharpened her determination to succeed. In the early mornings and late afternoons, Serena and her sister Venus practiced religiously under the watchful eye of their father, Richard Williams—a man with no formal tennis training but an unshakable vision. "You're going to be the greatest," Richard often told his daughters, his voice firm and full of conviction. "You just have to work harder than anyone else."

Her father's plan was bold, even audacious. After watching a tennis match on TV and reading tennis manuals from the local library, he decided that this was a sport that his daughters would conquer. He scribbled out a 78-page plan for their training, determined to make them champions. The neighborhood courts were terribly run down and littered with broken glass, a far cry from the pristine lawns of Wimbledon. But to Richard, they were more than enough. "If you can play here, you can play anywhere," he'd say, sweeping away debris before handing them their rackets.

Compton in the 1980s was tough. There was stifling economic hardship, a high crime rate and widespread gang violence. Gunshots sometimes pierced the stillness, making Serena flinch, but she never quit. Once, during a practice, a police helicopter circled low overhead, its spotlight momentarily blinding her. She had to shield her eyes with her racket. "It wasn't just practice—it was survival," she would later recall.

Though Richard was a constant figure on the sidelines, barking advice and pushing her to dig deeper, Serena's determination came from within. She wasn't just playing tennis—she was proving something to herself. "I always believed I was destined for this," she said years later. "I didn't care what anyone else thought."

Serena faced more battles beyond her neighborhood tennis courts. As a young black girl in a predominantly white sport, she endured sneers, dismissive comments and outright racism. "People looked at me like I didn't belong," she said, recalling her earliest tournaments. "But I always thought, 'Why not me? My dad always told me, 'They don't decide your story. You do.'"

When she won her first Grand Slam title at just 17 years old, defeating Martina Hingis at the 1999 US Open, it was more than a victory. It was a statement. Serena had arrived. "That win wasn't just for me," she reflected later. "It was for every little girl who was told she couldn't. I wanted them to see what was possible."

Serenas' professional career was legendary. With 23 Grand Slam singles titles, she stands as the Open Era record holder, surpassing the greatest names in tennis and etching her place in history. Her dominance extended to the Olympic stage, where she claimed four gold medals—three in doubles and one in singles. Serena's achievements span every playing surface, with seven Wimbledon titles, six US Open victories, seven Australian Open championships and three French Open wins, a testament to her unparalleled versatility and mastery of the game.

Even as Serena's career soared, she never forgot her roots. "Compton gave me my fire," she often said. "It taught me to fight for what I want and never to back down." Her story—woven with dedication, setbacks and triumphs—became an inspiration not just for athletes but for anyone daring to dream beyond their circumstances.

Lionel Messi's journey to soccer greatness began on the streets of Rosario, Argentina. "Leo could dribble before he could talk," his grandmother, Celia, often said with a laugh. She was his first and biggest fan, taking him to matches and reminding everyone, "This boy is special."

From a young age, Lionel Messi's talent on the soccer field was unmistakable. He effortlessly outmaneuvered opponents much larger than him, the ball seemingly a natural extension of his feet. Yet, at 11, a growth hormone deficiency threatened to halt his dreams—his family could hardly afford the necessary treatment. Undeterred, Messi's resolve only hardened. "I'll play anyway," he declared, embodying a spirit of determination that would define his journey.

A turning point came when FC Barcelona scouts witnessed Messi's extraordinary skills during a trial in Spain. Messi, just 13 years old, was a tiny figure on the pitch, dwarfed by the older boys trying out. But the moment he touched the ball, the scouts were spellbound. Every pass, every dribble, every shot seemed effortless. "Sign him," one scout reportedly told the club's director. "We may never see talent like this again."

However, Messi faced a significant hurdle: the costly medical treatment he needed for growth and development. FC Barcelona stepped in with an extraordinary offer to cover his treatment costs, provided he and his family moved to Spain. This opportunity meant leaving everything familiar behind—his friends, his neighborhood and his supportive grandmother, Celia. "Leaving was tough," Messi reflected, "but it was my shot at my dream." This move, challenging as it was, fueled his determination to reach his goal of professional soccer.

The transition to La Masia, Barcelona's esteemed football academy, was brutal. Dwarfed by his peers and unfamiliar with Spanish Catalan, he often found solace in calls home, expressing a longing to return. Yet, Messi transformed his homesickness into unyielding determination. His presence on the training ground, long after others had departed, was a testament to his resolve. Alone, he would practice tirelessly, the glow of the setting sun his only companion. Focusing on incremental goals—honing a specific shot, mastering intricate drills, refining his control with both feet—his dedication was palpable. This disciplined approach rapidly distinguished him, as his skill, strategic insight and persistence shone brightly.

At 17, Messi made his debut for Barcelona's first team, scoring his first goal with a flick so delicate and precise that even seasoned players stopped to applaud. It was the moment the world met Lionel Messi—the boy from Rosario who was destined for greatness. "That goal wasn't just for me," Messi later said. "It was for everyone who believed in me when the odds were against us."

Messi shattered records over the next two decades, winning numerous titles, including multiple UEFA Champions League and La Liga trophies and claimed seven Ballon d'Or awards. But the crowning moment came in 2022 when he led Argentina to victory in the FIFA World Cup, lifting the trophy as tears streamed down his face. "I've waited my whole life for this," he said, the culmination of a journey that began on those dusty streets in Rosario.

Messi's story is more than a tale of athletic greatness—it's a testament to resilience, sacrifice and the power of belief. From his parents' unshakable support to Barcelona's bold decision to invest in his future, Messi's rise reminds us that talent alone isn't enough. It takes grit, determination and the right opportunities to turn a dream into reality.

Serena Williams and Lionel Messi's journeys underscore perseverance's pivotal role. Serena combated racism and sexism through relentless practice and the unwavering support of her family, particularly her father Richard's fearless coaching. Messi, on the other hand, faced a daunting medical challenge and the task of acclimating to a new country at a young age, supported by FC Barcelona's faith in his abilities. Both athletes' stories exemplify overcoming adversity by never backing down, the belief in oneself and the importance of staying fixed on one's goals. Their paths reveal that true greatness and confidence are cultivated through facing and conquering challenges, showcasing the transformative power of perseverance and self-belief.

BREAKING THE MOLD: HOW SIMONE BILES AND MICHAEL PHELPS REDEFINED EXCELLENCE

Simone Biles and Michael Phelps are two athletes who didn't just compete in their sports; they redefined them. Simone Biles' ascent in gymnastics began in a modest gym in Spring, Texas, amid chalk dust clouds and the sound of gymnasts in motion. At six, her unstoppable energy and joy were evident. "She was always flipping," her mother, Nellie Biles, remembered. A coach, spotting Simone's raw talent, recommended gymnastics classes. Reflecting on that pivotal moment, Simone shared, "I knew I belonged in that gym."

Simone's early years in gymnastics were a whirlwind of progress. Coaches were astonished by her uncanny ability to twist and flip, her movements so fluid and powerful that she made the impossible look easy. "We'd never seen a kid like her," one coach remembered. "She didn't just do the drills—she owned them." Her love for the sport was evident in the way her face lit up after a perfect routine. "I loved flying," she said. "There's nothing like that feeling."

As she rose through the ranks, Simone proved she wasn't just another promising gymnast—she was a phenomenon. By her teens, her routines were rewriting the rules of gymnastics. In 2021, she performed the Yurchenko double pike—a vault so dangerous most gymnasts wouldn't dare attempt it. "I just thought, why not?" she said with a grin. When she nailed the landing, judges didn't have a name for it. Now they do: *The Biles*. "It's not just that she does the hardest skills," one commentator said. "It's how she does them—with joy, power and absolute control."

But Simone's success is rooted in resilience. Her early years were marked by instability, and she and her siblings were placed in foster care before being adopted by her grandparents, Nellie and Ron Biles. "They saved me," Simone often says. "They gave me the foundation to dream." That foundation carried her to incredible heights. By 2016, with 25 World Championship medals and four Olympic golds, she became the most decorated gymnast in history, captivating the world with her gravity-defying performances.

Yet Simone's greatest act of strength came during the 2021 Tokyo Olympics. She confronted the "twisties"—a gymnast's nightmare where one loses spatial awareness in mid-air, making every move dangerously unpredictable. It wasn't just her performance at risk—it was her safety. Amid the high-stakes competition, Simone made a groundbreaking decision: she withdrew from several events, including the individual all-around, a title she was favored to win.

Her choice sent shockwaves around the world. Critics questioned her resolve and commitment, but her decision resonated with a far larger audience. Simone sparked a global conversation about mental health and the immense pressures athletes face. "It wasn't worth the risk to my body and my mind," she explained. Her courage to prioritize her well-being over accolades was both revolutionary and inspiring.

"I had to listen to my body and my mind," she said. Her actions underscored a powerful message: even the world's most elite athletes are not immune to mental health struggles. By stepping back, Simone redefined what it means to be a champion. "Strong isn't just pushing through—it's knowing when to step back," she said.

Simone's decision transformed her into an emblem of mental health advocacy. Her willingness to speak openly about her struggles inspired millions to value their own well-being. "It's okay not to be okay," she emphasized. Simone showed the world that true greatness isn't measured solely by medals but by authenticity, self-care and the courage to inspire others. In Tokyo, Simone proved that listening to oneself—even on the biggest stage—is the ultimate act of strength.

Michael Phelps, nicknamed "The Baltimore Bullet," wasn't just born to swim—he was engineered for it. With his 6'4" frame, a wingspan longer than his height, size 14 feet that worked like flippers and double-jointed ankles that gave him a freakishly efficient kick, Phelps looked like something out of an aquatic laboratory. But what truly set him apart wasn't his body—it was his mind. "I didn't want to just win," Phelps once said. "I wanted to do something no one else had ever done."

Phelps first dove into the water at age seven, a lively kid with boundless energy and an ADHD diagnosis. While it's widely recognized that children with ADHD often struggle with focus, fewer people appreciate the unique strengths many of them possess, such as boundless energy, the ability to hyperfocus on activities they enjoy and exceptional resilience and adaptability. "I wasn't great at sitting still," he said with a laugh. "But in the pool, I felt like I could channel all of that." What began as a way to manage restless energy quickly became his life-defining passion.

At just 11, Phelps began training under coach Bob Bowman, known for his intense regimen. Bowman recognized Phelps' raw potential and remarked, "He was a blank canvas with limitless possibilities." The training was rigorous, involving up to three sessions daily and covering 50 miles of swimming per week. Phelps acknowledged, "Bob was tough, but it was all to prepare me to be the best."

Phelps' training regimen was extraordinary, requiring him to consume an astounding 12,000 calories daily—pancakes, pasta and pizzas were staples, not for pleasure but necessity. "It was about survival," he explained. His dedication to shaving milliseconds off his times was relentless. "Every hundredth of a second matters. Winning is in the preparation," Phelps often remarked. Yet, the intense demands of competition brought with it self-doubt and a sense of worth tied to victory. "Feeling like anything less than winning was a failure," he confessed.

The 2008 Beijing Olympics marked the moment the whole world was properly introduced to Michael Phelps. His goal? Eight gold medals in a single Games, breaking Mark Spitz's long-standing record. Each race felt like a high-stakes thriller. In the 100-meter butterfly, he trailed until the final stroke, lunging for the wall to win by an impossible 0.01 seconds—a margin smaller than a blink. The finish was so close it required a frame-by-frame review. "I don't think I've ever screamed louder," Phelps said about that moment. By the time he touched the wall for his eighth gold, the world was in awe. Phelps wasn't just a swimmer; he was a legend.

But behind the medals and records, Phelps battled inner demons. Swimming had been his sanctuary, a place where he could feel in control. But after the glory of the Olympics, the quiet moments became unbearable. "I went from the highest of highs to the lowest of lows," he admitted. Depression and substance abuse followed and at his darkest point, Phelps questioned if he even wanted to live.

In a brave move, Phelps openly sought help and shared his struggles, saying, "I realized I wasn't alone. " He aimed to ensure that others felt supported. His honesty initiated a worldwide dialogue on mental health, demonstrating that true strength lies not in victories but in self-honesty.

Simone and Michael redefined gymnastics and swimming through their extraordinary accomplishments. Biles, known for her dynamic performances, promoted inclusivity in gymnastics, encouraging athletes to surpass traditional expectations. Phelps, with his record-breaking achievements, exemplified the rewards of perseverance and commitment, inspiring swimmers to aim for new heights. Facing their own hurdles, Biles championed mental health awareness, breaking down societal stigmas, while Phelps leveraged his ADHD diagnosis to drive his success, transforming challenges into motivation. Their journeys underscore the essence of self-discovery and confidence, highlighting the value of self-awareness, the courage to defy norms and the pursuit of lofty aspirations. Their narratives prove that true excellence is not solely about triumphs but also about pioneering, motivating and converting obstacles into opportunities for personal growth.

UNCOVERING POTENTIAL: THE RISE OF MARCUS RASHFORD AND NAOMI OSAKA

Marcus Rashford's rise from the streets of Manchester to global prominence is a story of talent, determination and purpose. Born into a working-class family in Wythenshawe, Marcus grew up amidst strife and grit. His mother, Melanie, worked multiple low-paying jobs, often skipping meals to ensure her five children had something to eat. "Sometimes we didn't even have a loaf of bread in the house," Marcus recalled. Despite her sacrifices, he and his siblings often went to bed with the gnawing emptiness of hunger.

Melanie scraped together whatever she could to afford his football training, nurturing a passion Marcus discovered early on. On the field, Marcus often felt different from his teammates, many of whom came from more stable homes. Yet he channeled those feelings into relentless determination. "I wanted to make it —not just for me but for my mum and my family," he shared. These struggles shaped Marcus into not only an exceptional athlete but also a compassionate advocate for others facing similar challenges.

For Marcus, soccer was more than just his game—it was an escape and a purpose. From the moment he kicked a ball in the neighborhood park, his talent was undeniable. Coaches marveled at his quick thinking, dazzling footwork and steely confidence. "Marcus always had this focus," one early coach said. "Even then, you could see he wasn't just playing—he was chasing something bigger."

At seven, Marcus joined Manchester United's prestigious youth academy, a dream for any young player growing up in the shadow of Old Trafford. But the academy demanded discipline, sacrifice and obsessive commitment. While classmates worried about homework, Marcus pushed himself through grueling drills, always striving to improve. "I knew I had to grow up fast," Marcus said. "There wasn't room for excuses." The hours he poured into training weren't just about football—they were about honoring his family's sacrifices.

His dedication paid off in February 2016, when an injury crisis left Manchester United scrambling for players. At 18, Marcus was thrust into the starting lineup for a Europa League match against Midtjylland. It was a trial by fire—but Marcus rose to the occasion, scoring twice in front of a roaring Old Trafford crowd. "It was surreal," he said. "One minute, I'm just a kid dreaming of playing for United. The next, I'm living it."

Marcus repeated the feat three days later, scoring twice in his Premier League debut against Arsenal. The media dubbed him a teenage sensation but Marcus stayed grounded. "I just wanted to make my family proud," he said.

While his star rose on the pitch, Marcus never forgot his roots. Having experienced food insecurity as a child, he understood the pain of hunger. During the COVID-19 pandemic, when school closures left millions of children without free meals, Marcus launched a campaign to extend the program. "I know what it's like to go without," he said. "No child should ever have to feel that." His advocacy struck a chord, mobilizing public support and forcing a government U-turn that secured meals for millions of children. "My mum taught me to fight for what's right," he said, his voice cracking with emotion.

Marcus didn't stop there. He raised millions for charities, tackled education inequality and used his platform to inspire change. His efforts earned him an honorary doctorate and a spot on TIME's list of the 100 most influential people. Despite the accolades, Marcus remains humble. "I'm just a kid from Manchester trying to make a difference," he said.

Naomi Osaka's rise to tennis stardom had humble beginnings, far removed from the grand stages she would one day command. With a Haitian father and a Japanese mother, her multicultural background set her apart early in the competitive realm of tennis. Inspired by the trailblazing success of the Williams sisters, Naomi and her sister Mari practiced tirelessly on the deteriorated courts of Queens, New York, driven by their father Leonard François's firm belief in their potential. "If they can do it, so can my girls," Leonard asserted, instilling in Naomi a profound sense of purpose and belonging in the sport. Naomi herself acknowledges the significant influence Serena Williams had on her, considering her success a continuation of Williams' legacy, a testament to the enduring impact of role models in sports.

When Naomi 's family moved to Florida for her advanced training, her talent was undeniable. With a powerful serve and a quiet determination, Naomi stood out early on. Turning professional in 2013, her rise to fame accelerated in 2018 at the Indian Wells Open, securing her first major title. Yet, it was her win against Serena Williams at the U.S. Open the same year that truly defined her career. Facing her childhood idol, Naomi showcased her remarkable skill and toughness, clinching a victory that solidified her status in tennis and marked a significant milestone in her personal journey.

Facing the greatest player of all time, Naomi stepped onto the court with quiet determination. The crowd was electric. From the first serve, she unleashed blistering groundstrokes and pinpoint serves that left Serena, a player known for her dominance, scrambling to keep up. Naomi wasn't just playing well; she was outplaying her hero.

As the match progressed, the atmosphere tensed when a dispute between Serena and the umpire over a code violation turned the crowd's cheers into boos. Amidst this tumult, Osaka maintained her composure, focusing on the game. Her unshakeable concentration delivered a victory that crowned her the first Japanese player to win a Grand Slam title. Although the achievement was significant, the trophy presentation was overshadowed by the audience's reaction. Visibly emotional, Naomi expressed regret amid the turmoil, demonstrating her humility and grace. She conveyed gratitude for the victory but also sadness over the controversy, highlighting her deep respect for Serena.

Naomi's star continued to rise. By 2021, she had claimed four Grand Slam titles, including two Australian Opens and another U.S. Open. She became the first Asian player to achieve the world No. 1 ranking and became the highest-paid female athlete globally. But her impact extended far beyond the court.

In 2020, amid global protests against racial injustice, Naomi Osaka made headlines by wearing masks at the U.S. Open, each bearing the name of a victim of police violence, like Breonna Taylor and George Floyd. "I wanted to use my platform to bring awareness," she stated, transforming each game into a compelling plea for justice. The following year, Osaka again captured global attention at the 2021 French Open by withdrawing to focus on her mental health, citing anxiety and depression. "It's okay not to be okay," she courageously affirmed, challenging the stigma around mental health in sports. Her actions spurred a worldwide dialogue, encouraging a reevaluation of strength and prompting a more open conversation about the mental pressures athletes face.

Marcus Rashford and Naomi Osaka embody the transformative power of early talent recognition, resilience and nurturing guidance. Rising from adversity—Rashford's childhood poverty and Osaka's modest beginnings—they channeled their struggles into excellence, with Rashford becoming a Manchester United star and Osaka a global tennis icon. Beyond their athletic achievements, they have used their platforms to drive social change: Rashford campaigns against child food poverty, while Osaka advocates for racial justice and mental health. Their journeys illustrate self-discovery and confidence, highlighting how self-belief, community support and standing for one's values can inspire resilience and create meaningful impact.

INTERCONNECTING THE STORIES OF SELF-DISCOVERY AND CONFIDENCE OF THE SIX ATHLETES

In the arena of sports, as in life, confronting and overcoming adversity often opens a door to self-discovery and the development of confidence. Serena Williams, Lionel Messi, Simone Biles, Michael Phelps, Marcus Rashford and Naomi Osaka each navigated unique challenges, demonstrating that confidence is built not in the absence of fear but through the bravery to confront it. Serena and Messi exemplify resilience, turning societal and physical hurdles into milestones. Similarly, Biles and Phelps transcended the norms of their sports, championing mental health and redefining the essence of victory. Rashford and Osaka's endeavors off the field, advocating against child food poverty and for racial justice, illustrate the impact of leveraging one's platform for societal change. Their journeys reveal a common thread: the critical choice between succumbing to adversity or advancing despite it. Biles and Osaka, facing scrutiny for prioritizing mental health, illustrated that vulnerability is a form of courage that we don't honor enough. It empowers growth, connects people to us and encourages others to value their well-being. These stories impart invaluable lessons: the significance of resilience against discrimination from Serena, Messi's testament to perseverance, Biles's advocacy for redefining success, Phelps's transformation of weaknesses into strengths and Rashford and Osaka's proof that one's voice can catalyze meaningful change. Reflecting on these narratives prompts us to consider how we might navigate similar obstacles. They challenge us to think about our values and the impact of our choices. They teach us that the growth from self-discovery extends beyond triumphs; it's about the journey of overcoming, learning and evolving into our fullest selves.

————

PAUSE FOR A QUICK TIMEOUT! Let's step to the sideline for a moment to talk about journaling. I highly recommend picking up a journal to use alongside this book. It doesn't matter if it's a simple notebook or a fancy leather-bound one—whatever feels right for you works perfectly. Journaling is one of the most valuable tools for teenagers and it pairs beautifully with the lessons in this book. As you dive into these inspiring stories, your journal becomes a private space to reflect on what you've read, explore your thoughts and apply the lessons to your own life. It's where you can celebrate your successes, navigate challenges and set goals for the future—just like the athletes in these pages. Writing things down helps you process emotions, track your progress and discover your unique strengths. Over time, your journal evolves into your personal playbook for resilience, leadership, self-discovery and growth. Now, with your journal by your side, let's get back into the game!

————

REFLECTION: WHAT CHALLENGES ARE SHAPING YOU?

The athletes in this chapter remind us that confidence isn't innate; it's a skill shaped by our choices in the face of challenges. Each story highlights the power of resilience, vulnerability and action in personal growth. Use these questions to explore how you can find confidence in your own life:

• *Facing Fear:* Serena Williams and Lionel Messi encountered barriers that could have held them back—whether societal expectations or physical limitations. What fears or challenges do you face? Are there steps you can take to confront them with courage? Start by reflecting on these in your new journal.

• *Redefining Success:* Simone Biles and Michael Phelps challenged traditional ideas of success, prioritizing their well-being over medals. What does success mean to you? How can you define it in a way that reflects your personal values and priorities?

• *Using Your Voice:* Marcus Rashford and Naomi Osaka used their platforms to advocate for change. Think about a time when you stood up for something important. How can you use your unique skills and opportunities to make a difference in your community?

• *Learning Through Vulnerability:* Vulnerability, as taught by Simone and Naomi, isn't weakness—it's strength. Have you ever let yourself be vulnerable in pursuit of growth? How did it feel and what did you learn from the experience?

Take time to journal your answers. These reflections can help you connect with your inner strengths and chart a path toward greater confidence.

ACTION PLAN: BUILDING CONFIDENCE AND DISCOVERING YOURSELF

• *Identify a Personal Challenge:* Choose one challenge you're currently facing—whether it's a fear, a skill you want to develop or a difficult situation. Write down one small, specific step you can take this week to move toward overcoming it.

• *Redefine Success for Yourself:* Reflect on an area in your life where you feel pressure to meet external expectations. Create your own definition of success for that area—one that aligns with your values and personal growth, rather than comparison to others.

• *Practice Self-Compassion:* Confidence grows when we treat ourselves with kindness. Write down three affirmations that remind you of your strengths, such as "I am capable of learning," or "My effort is more important than perfection." Repeat them whenever you feel discouraged.

• *Take Action for Others:* Like Rashford and Osaka, look for one way you can make a difference in someone else's life. It might be as simple as helping a friend, speaking up for someone in need or volunteering for a cause you care about. Focusing on our impact on others often builds confidence.

• *Embrace Vulnerability:* Identify one area where you've been hesitant to show vulnerability. This might involve asking for help, sharing your feelings or admitting a mistake. Take one small step toward embracing vulnerability this week and notice how it strengthens your relationships and confidence.

• *Celebrate Progress, Not Perfection:* Keep a "Confidence Chapter" in your journal where you record one thing each day that you're proud of—big or small. Whether it's finishing a project, trying something new or simply getting through a tough day, celebrating progress helps reinforce self-belief.

• *Learn from Others:* Choose one athlete from this chapter whose story resonates most with you. Research more about their journey, challenges and growth. Write down one or two lessons you can apply to your own life.

• *Visualize Your Future Self:* Take a few minutes to imagine yourself in the future as a more confident, self-assured version of who you are today. Visualize how you'll handle challenges, interact with others and achieve your goals. This mental exercise can help reinforce your belief in your ability to grow.

A final thought: Confidence is a journey. The athletes in this chapter teach us that confidence isn't about being fearless—it's about showing up despite fear, growing through challenges and discovering the strength in vulnerability. Every choice you make to confront adversity, learn from setbacks and live authentically brings you closer to becoming your fullest self.

Take a step today, however small, toward embracing your own journey of self-discovery. Remember, confidence is built over time —one action, one reflection, one moment at a time.

2 RESILIENCE

AGAINST ALL ODDS: BETHANY HAMILTON AND OSCAR PISTORIUS' TRIUMPH OVER PHYSICAL BARRIERS

IMAGINE CARVING THROUGH A PERFECT WAVE, the ocean's power propelling you forward as sunlight dances on the water. Now, imagine doing it with only one arm. For Bethany Hamilton, this isn't just a challenge; it's her reality.

Growing up on the shores of Kauai, Hawaii, Bethany was born into the waves. Her parents were surfers and she was already catching her own by age five. "The ocean is my happy place," she said. By 13, Bethany was dominating local competitions with a style full of grace and fearlessness. Coaches and fans saw her as a rising star destined for professional surfing success.

But everything changed on Halloween morning in 2003. The day started like any other. Bethany paddled out with her best friend, Alana Blanchard and Alana's father and brother to catch the early waves before school. The water shimmered under the rising sun, calm and inviting. Bethany lay on her board, relaxing in the cool ocean as she chatted with Alana. The moment felt serene and peaceful.

Then, in an instant, it wasn't.

A flash of movement below. Before she could react, the water exploded in chaos as a 14-foot tiger shark struck, severing her left arm below the shoulder. Blood poured into the water, clouding it in a deep red haze. The shark's massive tail fin broke the surface momentarily before disappearing into the depths.

"I didn't feel pain right away," Bethany later said. "Just pressure, like a hard tug." But when she looked down her arm was gone. Blood was everywhere, swirling around her board and she knew she had only moments to act. "I thought, 'This is it. I'm not going to make it,'" she admitted.

Alana's father swiftly paddled to Bethany, who remained eerily calm. He pulled her onto his board, tying a tourniquet with a surfboard leash to slow the bleeding. Blood trailed behind them as they paddled to shore, every second feeling like an eternity. On the beach, Bethany lay pale and trembling. "Stay awake, Bethany," Alana begged as her father called for help.

At the hospital, Bethany's father, scheduled for his own knee surgery, watched in shock as his daughter was wheeled into the operating room originally assigned to him. She had lost over 60% of her blood but surgeons narrowly saved her. "The shark missed her vital arteries by inches," the surgeon said. "It's a miracle she survived." Doctors saved her life, but her world had been forever changed.

The weeks after the attack were filled with pain and doubt. Would she ever surf again? Deep down, Bethany knew the answer. "I never saw myself giving up surfing," she said. Less than a month later, she was back in the ocean. Her first attempts were humbling. "I'd wipe out more than I'd stand up," she admitted. But day by day, she adapted, building the strength, balance and courage to ride again.

Bethany's resilience didn't just get her back on the board—it propelled her to greatness. In 2005, just two years after the attack, she won a national surfing title, proving that no obstacle could hold her back. By 17, she turned pro, competing against the best in the world. Her powerful, aggressive style made her a standout in competitions, but her humility and unwavering faith won hearts off the water.

Her story didn't stop with surfing. Bethany shared her journey in her bestselling autobiography, *Soul Surfer*, which was later adapted into a Hollywood film. As a motivational speaker and advocate, she has inspired millions, urging them to face life's challenges with grit and grace. "I don't need easy," Bethany once said. "I just need possible."

Born in South Africa without fibulae in both legs, Oscar Pistorius faced a life that many would have seen as defined by limitation. At just 11 months old, his parents made the gut-wrenching decision to have both of their son's legs amputated below the knees. It was a bold move but one made with hope. "It's not about what he's missing," his mother, Sheila, wrote in a note pinned to his bedroom wall. "It's about what he has."

From the start, Oscar was determined to prove she was right. As a child, he was fearless. Strapped into his first pair of prosthetics, he took his first steps with a wobble—and then broke into a run. Whether chasing his brother around the garden or kicking a soccer ball, Oscar threw himself into everything. "Those blades didn't slow me down—they sped me up," he later said.

In his teenage years, Oscar's energy was boundless. He played rugby with ferocity, but a knee injury during a match led him to track and field for rehabilitation. "The first time I put on sprinting blades it was like I was flying," he said. His natural speed was evident immediately and coaches quickly realized this wasn't just talent—it was groundbreaking.

Oscar's rise was meteoric. At 17, he stunned the world at the

2004 Athens Paralympics, winning gold in the 200-meter sprint and setting a world record. "I realized then," he said, "that I wasn't just running for myself—I was running to show the world what's possible."

But dominating the Paralympics wasn't enough. "I wanted to prove that I could compete with the best," he said. His dream of running against able-bodied athletes wasn't just ambitious—it was revolutionary.

This goal came with hurdles. Critics argued that his prosthetic blades gave him an unfair mechanical advantage. The debate intensified in 2008 when the International Association of Athletics Federations (IAAF) ruled that he couldn't compete in the Olympics. "It felt like they weren't just saying no to me—they were saying no to everyone like me," Oscar said.

Refusing to accept the decision, Oscar fought back. After months of biomechanical testing, the Court of Arbitration for Sport overturned the ban, clearing the way for him to compete against the world's best.

In 2012, Oscar made history as the first double-amputee sprinter to compete in the London Olympics. The stadium roared as he lined up for the 400-meter heat, his blades flexing at the line. "The crowd's noise was deafening but all I could hear was my heartbeat," he said. Though he didn't medal, advancing to the semifinals was a victory that transcended the race. His performance shattered stereotypes, showing that athletes with disabilities could compete on the world's biggest stage.

But Oscar's story took a dark and tragic turn in 2013. The world was shocked when he was charged with the murder of his girlfriend, Reeva Steenkamp. The details of the case were chilling and the trial dominated headlines, overshadowing his once-celebrated career. His conviction turned him from a global icon of perseverance into a figure of controversy, forever complicating his legacy.

Despite the complexities of his story, Oscar Pistorius' impact on sports remains undeniable. He forced the world to reconsider the limits of human potential, inspiring countless others to chase their dreams no matter the odds. His journey—marked by triumph and tragedy—is a testament to the heights and depths of the human spirit.

Bethany Hamilton and Oscar Pistorius exemplify resilience through their remarkable comebacks from extreme physical adversity. Bethany, after a shark attack left her with one arm, ingeniously adapted her surfing technique, demonstrating an unyielding spirit. Oscar, the "Blade Runner," defied the odds by racing on prosthetic legs, redefining athletic possibilities for those with disabilities. Both athletes showcased not just physical resilience but a mental toughness supported by their communities and families. Their journeys teach a critical lesson: true resilience is built on confronting challenges directly, drawing strength from setbacks and relentlessly pursuing goals, no matter the obstacles.

RISING FROM THE ASHES: THE COMEBACK STORIES OF ANDRE AGASSI AND LINDSEY VONN

Andre Agassi wasn't just a tennis player; he was a rebel, a showman and an icon who changed how the world saw the sport. With his neon outfits, wild mane of hair and cocky swagger, Agassi captivated millions. On the court, his blistering baseline game and laser-like return of serve made him a force to be reckoned with. But behind the flash was a man wrestling with pressure, personal demons and a deep ambivalence toward the game that defined his life.

Born in Las Vegas, Agassi grew up under the watchful eye of his demanding father, Mike, a former boxer turned tennis fanatic. Mike saw tennis not as a game but as a ticket to greatness for his son. Grueling sessions on their backyard court, nicknamed "The Dragon," were relentless. A custom-built ball machine spat out hundreds of balls daily, drilling Andre with military precision. "I didn't ask to play tennis. It was my father's dream. That's where the trouble started," Agassi later wrote. "I tried because I thought maybe if I was good enough, he'd stop."

By 13, Andre's talent earned him a spot at Nick Bollettieri's renowned tennis academy in Florida. For most, it would be a dream come true, but for Andre, it felt like a prison. The strict routines, grueling practices and bare-bones dorm rooms left him miserable. "It wasn't a school—it was a boot camp. But I didn't have a choice," he confessed. Yet his talent grew. At 16, Andre turned pro, stepping into a world that demanded perfection. Crowds adored his electric baseline game, but inside he was conflicted. "Tennis was my ticket out. I didn't choose this life but I had to figure out how to live it."

Agassi's rise in the late 1980s was meteoric. With his rebellious image—denim shorts, long hair and anti-establishment attitude— he became a pop culture sensation. Critics called him hype without a Grand Slam title to back it up. That changed in 1992 at Wimbledon. Agassi, once mocked for skipping the tournament due to its dress code, silenced doubters by winning. He fell to his knees in triumph, tears streaming down his face. "For once," he said, "I felt like I belonged."

Over the next decade, Agassi earned eight Grand Slam titles and completed a Career Grand Slam. Yet success masked his inner turmoil. Fame, relentless pressure and injuries weighed on him. "I hated tennis," Agassi admitted in his memoir *Open*. By the late 1990s, his ranking fell to No. 141 and personal struggles drove him to substance abuse. "I felt like I was falling into a black hole," he said.

At rock bottom, Agassi chose to fight back. With coach Brad Gilbert's guidance, he overhauled his mindset and game. "It wasn't about flash anymore," he said. "It was about grit." In one of tennis' greatest comebacks, he won the 1999 French Open to complete his Career Grand Slam and reclaimed the No. 1 ranking. "Winning that French Open taught me I could face anything."

Off the court, Agassi found balance. "When I stopped trying to be perfect, I found joy again." After a failed marriage to actress Brooke Shields, he married tennis legend Steffi Graf. Together, they focused on family and philanthropy, raising millions through the Andre Agassi Foundation for Education to support under-privileged children. "Winning is great, but it's temporary," Agassi said. "Building something that lasts—that's what really matters."

Lindsey Vonn's story is a testament to toughness, endurance and an unyielding will to conquer whatever life throws her way. Widely regarded as one of the greatest ski racers in history, her journey to the pinnacle of her sport was anything but smooth. From her humble beginnings on the slopes of Minnesota to the treacherous runs of the World Cup circuit, Lindsey's path was marked by extraordinary highs and brutal lows.

Lindsey's love for skiing began as a child. "I could barely walk but I wanted to ski," she once recalled. Her parents bundled her up in oversized gear and set her loose on the gentle hills of Buck Hill, Minnesota. Under the guidance of Erich Sailer, a legendary ski coach, Lindsey's potential was evident early on. Even then, she wasn't just fast—she was fearless. "She wasn't afraid of falling; she was afraid of not going fast enough," Sailer said.

At 15, Lindsey moved with her family to Vail, Colorado, to chase bigger dreams. The transition was tough—a new school, a new environment—but her focus never wavered. By her late teens, Lindsey was competing internationally, earning her first World Cup victory in 2004 at just 20 years old. "Winning that race was everything I'd worked for," she said. "But I knew it was just the beginning."

Ski racing, however, is punishing. Lindsey's career became a stark reminder of the sport's dangers. She endured injuries that would have sidelined most athletes: torn ACLs, fractures, concussions and a shattered arm. Her crash at the 2013 World Championships in Schladming, Austria, was one of the most harrowing moments of her career. Known for her aggressive style, Lindsey pushed the limits of speed and control. Midway through the super-G course, her balance faltered after hitting soft snow. She launched into the air, twisted unnaturally and crashed violently onto her right leg.

The impact was devastating. Lindsey tumbled down the slope, skis flying in different directions. Spectators watched in horror as she lay motionless. "I knew something was seriously wrong the moment I hit the ground," she later said. The crash tore her ACL and MCL and fractured her tibial plateau—a brutal combination of injuries for any athlete, especially an elite skier. "It felt like my knee just exploded," she recalled.

Her road to recovery was grueling. Hours of physical therapy turned into months, filled with pain, setbacks and doubt. "There were days I wanted to quit," she admitted. "But skiing is who I am. I wasn't ready to give it up." Just as she prepared to return, another reinjury forced her back into surgery. Yet Lindsey refused to let adversity define her. "One step at a time. Just keep moving forward," she told herself.

Her comeback in 2015 was nothing short of extraordinary. Lindsey returned to the slopes with the same fire that had fueled her as a child. Over the next few years, she shattered records, ultimately becoming the most decorated female skier in history with 82 World Cup victories. Her wins were proof of her resilience and refusal to back down.

Beyond the medals, Lindsey became a symbol of perseverance. She spoke openly about her struggles with injuries and mental health, using her platform to inspire others. In 2019, Lindsey retired, her body finally signaling it was time. Yet retirement didn't mean slowing down. She became an advocate for mental health, a mentor to young athletes and an author, sharing her story to empower others. "The mountains will always be there," Lindsey often says. "What matters is how you climb them."

Andre Agassi and Lindsey Vonn embody resilience, each navigating their unique hurdles toward remarkable comebacks. Agassi's journey through self-doubt to tennis triumph underlines the importance of determination and mentorship. Meanwhile, Vonn's relentless battle against injury to remain atop the skiing world showcases true champion's grit. Their stories impart a crucial message: resilience lies in confronting challenges and transforming them into avenues for personal growth. They inspire us to harness Vonn's fire and Agassi's courage to redefine our own paths. Their commitment extends beyond their athletic feats; Agassi's educational initiatives and Vonn's advocacy work highlight their dedication to nurturing resilience and growth in others. Their narratives encourage us to view resilience not only as a defense against hardship but as a proactive pursuit of our highest ambitions.

DEFYING EXPECTATIONS: TOM BRADY'S DETERMINATION AND MONICA SELES' COURAGE

Tom Brady's journey is the ultimate underdog story—one of relentless determination, discipline and a will to succeed that redefined possibility. Drafted 199th overall in the sixth round of the 2000 NFL Draft, Brady was far from anyone's idea of a star. Grainy footage of his combine performance showed an awkward, slow-footed athlete—a stark contrast to the explosive quarterbacks dominating the league. One analyst quipped, "He looks like someone who should be selling insurance, not playing football."

But Brady knew differently. "They overlooked me," he later said, "but I knew what I was capable of."

Growing up in San Mateo, California, Brady idolized 49ers legend Joe Montana, often sitting in the stands at Candlestick Park with his dad, dreaming of leading a team to glory. "That's going to be me one day," he'd say. At Michigan, his path was far from easy. Brady spent two years as a backup, fighting for every snap. "Nothing was ever handed to me," he said.

When the Patriots drafted Brady, he arrived as a fourth-string quarterback and a long shot to make the team. But from day one, Brady exuded self-confidence. During his first meeting with owner Robert Kraft, he shook his hand firmly and said, "Hi, I'm Tom Brady. And I'm the best decision this organization has ever made." Kraft later admitted, "You couldn't help but believe him."

Brady's relentless work ethic backed up his words. He outworked everyone, studying playbooks late into the night. "He didn't have the strongest arm or the fastest legs," a teammate said, "but he had the strongest will."

In 2001, fate intervened. When starting quarterback Drew Bledsoe suffered a devastating injury, the Patriots turned to their untested backup. Brady stepped in with signature composure, proving week after week that he belonged. By the playoffs, he was fully in command.

The defining moment came at Super Bowl XXXVI. The Patriots faced the heavily favored St. Louis Rams, led by star quarterback Kurt Warner. Most analysts dismissed New England but Brady had other plans. With the game tied late in the fourth quarter, he orchestrated a masterful drive, methodically moving the ball downfield. "I wasn't thinking about the pressure," Brady said. "I was thinking about what needed to be done, one play at a time."

As time expired, kicker Adam Vinatieri nailed a 48-yard field goal, sealing a 20-17 victory and the Patriots' first Super Bowl title. The football world was stunned—a sixth-round pick had just toppled one of the league's greatest teams. At 24, Brady became the youngest quarterback to win a Super Bowl. His ability to deliver under pressure launched one of the greatest dynasties in NFL history. "That game gave me the confidence to believe I could win at the highest level," Brady reflected.

Brady's career wasn't without adversity. In 2008, a torn ACL sidelined him for the season but he attacked recovery with singular focus, returning stronger. "Injury is just a detour," he said.

In 2020, at 43, Brady shocked the NFL by leaving New England to join the struggling Tampa Bay Buccaneers. Critics doubted him, but Brady led the Bucs to a Super Bowl victory in his first season, earning his seventh championship—more than any NFL franchise.

Brady's legacy is unmatched. He revolutionized the quarterback position, breaking records for Super Bowl wins, touchdown passes and MVP awards. "If you're going to compete," he said, "why not aim to be the best?"

Monica Seles wasn't just an astounding young tennis player; she was a game-changer who recalibrated the sport with her power, passion and fearless intensity. Born in Novi Sad, Yugoslavia, Monica's love for tennis began in her family's tiny apartment, where her father, Karolj, would sketch tennis courts on the wall. "Aim for the lines," he'd tell her as Monica practiced swinging at imaginary balls with a fierceness that would define her game. By the time she was nine, she was winning junior tournaments, her two-handed forehand and backhand bewildering opponents. "From the start, she hit harder than anyone her age," Karolj proudly recalled.

At 13, Monica moved to Florida to train at the intense Nick Bollettieri Tennis Academy. The transition was difficult—she missed home and struggled with English—but her work ethic never wavered. "Every time I hit a ball," Monica said, "I imagined winning a Grand Slam." At 16, she made it a reality, winning the 1990 French Open and becoming the youngest champion in history. Her powerful baseline game and ferocious groundstrokes left opponents stunned. By 1991, she was dominating women's tennis, winning three of the four Grand Slam titles that year. Her grunts and piercing focus became her signature. "Every shot felt like it came with a purpose," recalled fellow star Mary Joe Fernández.

Her rivalry with Steffi Graf captivated fans worldwide, culminating in epic battles for many Grand Slam titles. But while Steffi was elegant and methodical, Monica was raw and emotional. By 1993, she held the world No. 1 ranking, amassing nine Grand Slam titles by the age of 19! She was unstoppable—or so it seemed.

On April 30, 1993, the unthinkable happened—a bizarre moment of horror that shook the world of sports. During a quarterfinal match at The Citizen Cup in Hamburg, Germany, Monica was dominating the game as usual and took a second set break. But as she walked to her chair, a man suddenly sprang from the stands, his movements quick and calculated, and plunged a nine-inch knife deeply into her back.

Seles let out a sharp scream and collapsed forward, clutching near her shoulder blade. Her shirt darkened as blood began to seep. Gasps erupted from the stunned crowd. Players and officials were frozen in shock. "I thought I was going to die," Monica later recounted, the memory of the searing pain still vivid. Blood soaked her tennis top as she lay on the court, dazed, the world spinning.

The attacker, a deranged Steffi Graf fanatic, was wrestled to the ground by security. His motive? A twisted desire to eliminate Monica as a rival to his idol, Steffi Graf. The attack was not just a violent assault but an act of madness that left the sports world reeling. In a shocking turn, the assailant walked free, receiving only a suspended sentence. Monica was devastated. "The justice system failed me," she said later, her voice heavy with emotion.

The knife narrowly missed her spinal cord and vital organs,

and while the physical wound healed, the emotional scars were far deeper. The attack shattered her sense of safety, leaving Monica battling fear, betrayal and a loss of trust. What should have been a milestone in her career became a nightmare that haunted her for years. She withdrew from tennis for over two years, grappling with depression and questioning if she'd ever return. Yet, deep down, her fighting spirit refused to give up.

In 1995, Monica made a triumphant return. Her first tournament back was the Canadian Open, where she stunned the tennis world by winning the title. Fans greeted her with overwhelming love, a moment she described as "like coming home." Then, in 1996, she claimed her ninth Grand Slam title at the Australian Open. Though she never regained the dominance of her early years, Monica's resilience was undeniable. "It wasn't just about winning anymore," she said. "It was about proving to myself that I could rise again."

Monica Seles' story transcends her nine Grand Slam titles. By openly sharing her struggles with mental health and fear, she became a beacon of hope and fortitude. Her courage in the face of unimaginable adversity inspired countless fans. "It's not about how many matches you win," she said. "It's about how many times you get back up."

Tom Brady rose above being consistently underestimated, while Monica Seles faced the daunting challenge of recovering from a shocking injury. Brady's disciplined confidence and mental fortitude highlight the power of a proactive mindset in overcoming skepticism or injury, while Seles's journey through the emotional aftermath of her trauma underscores the critical role of mental health in recovery. Brady's rise and Seles's extraordinary comeback embody not only athletic robustness but also a profound resilience that bridges both physical and emotional strength. Together, their stories reveal that resilience, forged through discipline and emotional tenacity, is essential for triumph and growth.

INTERCONNECTING THE RESILIENCE STORIES OF OUR SIX ATHLETES

Resilience is a vibrant thread that connects each story in this chapter, highlighting the journey from adversity to growth. Bethany Hamilton and Oscar Pistorius exemplify overcoming physical challenges with a spirit that refuses to be defined by barriers. Their remarkable adaptations in the face of life-altering events showcase resilience as a journey forward not just a rebound. Andre Agassi and Lindsey Vonn's experiences reveal resilience in confronting personal and physical struggles. Agassi's battle with his inner demons and Vonn's relentless fight through career-threatening injuries underscore the importance of perseverance and the willingness to embrace change as integral steps on the path to success. Tom Brady and Monica Seles demonstrate the mental fortitude required to overcome doubt, fear and trauma. Brady's disciplined approach to his play and recovery and Seles's courage in returning to tennis post-attack highlight the interplay between mental and physical endurance, emphasizing the holistic approach needed to tackle life's challenges. Reflect on these athletes' stories and consider how their decisions to seek help, challenge norms or find new ways to compete represent growth. Their journeys inspire us to view obstacles as opportunities for learning and self-discovery. Beyond sports, these narratives teach valuable life lessons on resilience. They show us the power of adversity to bolster strength, the importance of belief in oneself and the value of support networks. Let these stories motivate you to tackle your challenges with a positive mindset and a determination never to give in.

———

Personal Reflections on Building Back Better

Building resilience is more than just bouncing back from setbacks; it's about growing stronger with each challenge. To help you develop your resilience, consider starting with personal reflections. Think about these reflective questions as your starting point:

• *Overcoming Barriers:* Look back on a time when you faced a challenge that seemed insurmountable. How did you respond? Did you adapt or lean on someone for support like Bethany Hamilton finding a new way to surf or Oscar Pistorius proving his capabilities on the track? Did you try something else? What might you do differently next time?

• *Inner Struggles:* Andre Agassi battled with his inner doubts and a love-hate relationship with tennis. Are there areas in your life where internal conflicts hold you back? What steps can you take to address these feelings? Is there someone in your life with whom you can discuss your feelings?

• *Courage in Adversity:* Monica Seles had to summon incredible bravery to return to tennis after her attack. How do you handle fear or trauma in your life? Can you recall a moment when you had to summon courage to go forward? What did you learn about yourself in the process?

• *Support Systems:* Resilience isn't built alone. Whether it's a coach, friend, family member or mentor, support networks are key. Who are the people in your life who encourage you to keep going? Can you be completely honest and vulnerable with them? How can you strengthen these connections?

• *Mindset Shift:* Tom Brady's disciplined approach to proving everyone wrong shows the power of mental focus and unwavering self-belief. Have you ever felt underestimated? How might a change in perspective help you approach a current struggle of yours? Write down details of what a positive mindset would look like in your situation. How might you intensify your focus on a specific challenge if you decided to pursue it?

Take a few moments to journal your thoughts on these questions. Reflecting on your own experiences can help you see where resilience has already been a part of your life and where it can be cultivated further.

ACTION PLAN: CRAFTING RESILIENCE IN YOUR LIFE

• *Set a Small Goal:* Choose one area of your life where you're facing a challenge. Break it down into small, manageable steps. For example, if you're struggling with a subject in school, commit to asking for help from a teacher and studying for just 20 minutes a day. Track your progress and celebrate small victories—every step forward counts.

• *Adopt a Growth Mindset:* Write down one or two ways you can view challenges as opportunities. For instance, instead of saying, "I can't do this," replace it with, "I can learn how to do this." Post these affirmations where you can see them daily.

• *Build a Resilience Routine:* Incorporate habits that strengthen your resilience. These could include regular physical exercise, mindfulness or meditation or setting aside time daily to focus on gratitude. Take inspiration from Lindsey Vonn, who made a routine out of daily physical therapy to recover from injuries. Think of one habit you can add to your life starting today and make the commitment to yourself never to skip it.

• *Strengthen Your Support Network:* Identify three people you can lean on for encouragement. These might include family, friends, coaches or teachers. Reach out to them this week, whether by sharing your goals, asking for advice or just catching up. Remember, resilience grows in the presence of support, as it did for Monica Seles after her attack.

• *Learn from the Stories:* Pick one athlete from this chapter whose story resonates most with you. Write a short reflection on why their journey inspires you and what lessons you can apply to your own life.

• *Practice Self-Compassion:* Resilience doesn't mean being perfect or never feeling defeated. Give yourself grace when things are hard. When you stumble, remind yourself that it's part of the process, just as every athlete in this chapter faced setbacks on their journey.

By taking time to reflect and act on these lessons, you're not just reading about resilience—you're living it. Remember, resilience isn't something you're born with; it's a skill you build through experience, reflection and choice. Take your first steps today and keep moving forward, one small victory at a time.

3 LEADERSHIP AND CHARACTER BUILDING

LEADING BY EXAMPLE: THE INSPIRING LEADERSHIP OF LEBRON JAMES AND ABBY WAMBACH

PICTURE THIS: Game 7 of the NBA Finals. The Cleveland Cavaliers are locked in a battle with the Golden State Warriors, one of the most dominant teams in NBA history. Every dribble reverberates like a heartbeat, the championship hanging in the balance. All eyes are on LeBron James—"King James"—not just the face of basketball but a symbol of perseverance, leadership and hope. His journey from a challenging childhood in Akron, Ohio, to the pinnacle of the sport is a story of grit, greatness and the ability to inspire.

LeBron James's journey to greatness started in a small apartment he shared with his mother, Gloria. Facing hardship, they moved frequently, seeking stability wherever they could. Amid these challenges, basketball emerged as LeBron's refuge, a path to a future he could shape. Recognized early for his exceptional talent and understanding of the game, LeBron found both a mentor and a temporary home with Coach Frankie Walker, who nurtured his skills and instilled a profound appreciation for community. LeBron learned early on, "It's not about where you're from—it's about what you do with it," a principle that would guide his journey to becoming a basketball legend and a community leader.

By his high school years at St. Vincent-St. Mary, LeBron was a force on the court, capturing national attention. Dubbed "The Chosen One" by *Sports Illustrated*, he saw pressure as an opportunity, not a burden. Despite the awe his athletic prowess inspired—marked by spectacular dunks and smart plays—navigating fame at a young age was a challenge. "I was just a kid trying to figure it all out," LeBron admitted amidst the high expectations.

Selected first by the Cleveland Cavaliers in 2003, LeBron James shouldered an entire city's aspirations. "It wasn't merely about the game," he reflected. "It was about bringing hope to Cleveland." His unparalleled skill and leadership revitalized the team. "True leadership," LeBron noted, "is demonstrating what can be achieved, not issuing commands." During his time with the Cavaliers, James was pivotal in elevating the team from a struggling franchise to a dominant force in the NBA.

The defining chapter of his career came in 2016. Facing the 73-win Warriors in the Finals, the Cavaliers fell into a 3-1 deficit. No team had ever come back from such odds, but LeBron refused to back down. "We're not done yet," he told his teammates. His back-to-back 41-point performances in Games 5 and 6 were legendary, setting the stage for Game 7—a battle for the ages.

With less than two minutes left and the game tied, Andre Iguodala broke away for what seemed like a sure layup. LeBron, sprinting as a man possessed, launched his huge frame through the air and delivered the now-iconic chase-down block, pinning Iguodala's shot against the backboard. "I knew I had to make that play," he said. Moments later, Kyrie Irving's clutch three-pointer sealed the victory. As tears streamed down LeBron's face, he clutched the trophy and shouted: *"Cleveland, this is for you!"*—giving a long-suffering city its first championship in 52 years.

Off the court, LeBron's leadership is just as impactful. In 2018, he opened the I PROMISE School in Akron, offering at-risk children education, meals, transportation and free college tuition. "I've been in their shoes," he said. "I want these kids to know someone believes in them." LeBron is also a fierce advocate for social justice. In 2020, he co-founded *More Than a Vote* to fight voter suppression, helping thousands of marginalized voters access the polls. "Leadership means standing for what's right, even when it's uncomfortable," he said. "I've been blessed with a platform. And it's my responsibility to use it to make a difference."

Abby Wambach, soccer star, is a force of nature, a leader whose ferocity and passion defined every moment she spent on the field. Known for her uncanny ability to rise to the occasion, Abby carved her name into soccer history as one of the most prolific and clutch goalscorers ever. With 184 international goals—more than any player ever, male or female—her legacy isn't just in numbers but in the unforgettable moments of leadership that inspired millions.

Abby's soccer journey began in Rochester, New York, as the youngest of seven siblings in a competitive, sports-loving family. "We didn't play for fun; we played to win," Abby said, recalling backyard games often ending in scraped knees and fierce debates. That fiery spirit carried her to the University of Florida, where she dominated collegiate soccer, becoming the school's all-time leading scorer and earning a national championship. Even then, her coach described her as "a player who could change the course of a game in an instant."

Abby's defining moment came in the 2011 Women's World Cup quarterfinal against Brazil—a game teetering on the edge of disaster for the U.S. team. Trailing 2-1 in extra time, with seconds left on the clock, defeat seemed inevitable. The weight of elimination hung heavy in the air. Then, as if scripted for the movies, winger Megan Rapinoe unleashed a soaring cross from near midfield—a desperate, last-gasp attempt to keep their hopes alive.

Abby charged forward like a force of nature, her eyes locked on the ball as it arced into the box. She surged through a sea of defenders, her determination lifting her above the crowd. Suspended in the air, she met the ball with a thunderous header that rocketed past the goalkeeper and into the net. The stadium exploded in chaos—fans screaming, teammates collapsing in disbelief. Abby landed and raised her fists, her roar echoing through the arena. "I just remember thinking, 'We're not done yet,'" she said later, her voice still tinged with the fire of that moment.

The goal didn't just tie the game—it reignited the team. The U.S. went on to win in a penalty shootout and Abby's header instantly became one of the most iconic moments in soccer history. It was a testament to her resilience, unshakable belief and uncanny ability to deliver when everything was on the line.

Abby's greatness wasn't just about the goals; it was about her leadership. On the field, she was the heart and soul of her teams, rallying her teammates with her fiery words and unyielding determination. "Abby had this way of making you believe you were capable of anything," said a former teammate. Whether she was barking encouragement or leading by example with her tireless work ethic, Abby united her teams with a shared vision of victory.

Her leadership extended far beyond the pitch, becoming a cornerstone of her legacy. Abby has been a relentless advocate for gender equality, famously declaring, "We're not asking for favors; we're asking for fairness." She played a pivotal role in women's soccer's fight for equal pay, joining her teammates to file lawsuits, organize campaigns and demand justice. Her willingness to take on powerful institutions inspired a global movement for change, sparking crucial conversations about fairness in sports and beyond. "If we don't fight for ourselves, who will?" she asked, emphasizing the importance of collective action.

As an outspoken supporter of LGBTQ+ rights, Abby has used her platform to advocate for inclusion and acceptance, challenging stereotypes and encouraging authenticity. "Love and authenticity are the most powerful forms of activism," she said, reflecting her belief in creating change through courage and connection. Whether addressing inequality in sports or broader social justice issues, Abby has ensured her voice is heard, making her an advocate far beyond athletics.

Abby's influence reaches the next generation, encouraging young athletes to use their platforms for meaningful change. "Leadership is about standing up for what's right, even when it's hard," she has said—a mantra she lives daily. By advocating for equality and inclusion, Abby Wambach has shown that leadership is not just about personal success, but using that position to empower others and drive lasting progress.

LeBron James and Abby Wambach showcase distinct leadership styles, yet both share a commitment to their values and the ability to inspire change under pressure. LeBron's knack for uniting his teammates and leveraging their strengths mirrors Abby's focus on motivating her team and fighting for equality. Their paths underscore that true leadership always includes action. Both athletes demonstrate that leading effectively involves more than just holding a position of authority; it's about setting an example, valuing the uniqueness of each individual and pushing others to achieve their best

SILENT LEADERS: THE QUIET STRENGTH OF KAWHI LEONARD AND STEFFI GRAF

Kawhi Leonard is the embodiment of quiet dominance. His journey from an unassuming prospect to one of the NBA's most feared players is a story of relentless focus, a disciplined work ethic and an unshakable commitment to excellence. Known for his stoic demeanor and meticulous approach, Kawhi has never needed words to command attention—his game speaks volumes.

Kawhi Leonard's journey to basketball prominence began quietly on the courts of Riverside, California. Overshadowed by more conspicuous talents, he was a study in diligence. "He wasn't loud or flashy. He just worked tirelessly," his high school coach remembered. At 16, Kawhi faced a profound tragedy—the murder of his father, who owned a local car wash. This loss deeply affected him, yet it also fueled a deep-seated resolve. Kawhi found solace in basketball, a connection to his father that drove him forward. "Basketball became my escape. It felt like I was closer to my dad every time I played," he reflected.

At San Diego State, Kawhi's persistent hard work and defensive tenacity caught the attention of NBA scouts, though few predicted his meteoric rise. Selected 15th overall in the 2011 NBA Draft by the Indiana Pacers and quickly traded to the San Antonio Spurs, Kawhi joined a franchise known for nurturing talent. Under the mentorship of Gregg Popovich and the Spurs' veteran core, he transformed from a defensive specialist into a complete two-way player.

Kawhi Leonard's breakout moment arrived on the grandest stage—the 2014 NBA Finals. Tasked with guarding LeBron James, Kawhi faced an impossible challenge: shutting down the league's most dominant player. But Kawhi didn't just contain LeBron; he thoroughly disrupted him. Game after game, his relentless defense forced turnovers, altered shots and frustrated James. On the offensive end, Kawhi quietly chipped away at the Miami Heat's defenses. The Spurs dismantled the reigning champions in five games, claiming the title. At just 22 years old, Kawhi was named Finals MVP. "We saw the future of the NBA in this series," said Popovich. Ever humble, Kawhi deflected the praise: "I was just doing my job," he said, his modesty masking the magnitude of his achievement.

If the 2014 Finals announced Kawhi's arrival, Game 7 of the 2019 Eastern Conference Semifinals cemented his legend. With seconds left and the Toronto Raptors tied against the Philadelphia 76ers, the ball was in Kawhi's hands. With defenders swarming, he sprinted to the corner, rising above the chaos to release a high-arcing shot that hung in the air forever.

The ball bounced on the rim four times—time suspended—before dropping in. The arena erupted into chaos as Kawhi stayed crouched on the sideline, eyes locked on the rim, absorbing the slow-motion scene. It became an instant classic—the first Game 7 buzzer-beater in NBA history. "I just trusted my mechanics," Kawhi said afterward, calm as ever. That shot didn't just advance the Raptors; it was the moment that defined him—steady under fire, precise in execution and unshakable under pressure.

In the 2019 NBA Finals, Kawhi led the Raptors to their first-ever championship, dismantling the Golden State Warriors and earning his second Finals MVP award. His elite defense, clutch shooting and quiet leadership under immense pressure solidified his legacy as one of the game's greats. "Kawhi's not just a player—he's a force," said one teammate. "When he's locked in, nothing shakes him."

Off the court, Kawhi's mystique only adds to his legend, avoiding the spotlight, shunning social media and media antics. While others chase fame, Kawhi focuses solely on perfecting his craft: calmness, precision and winning. "I don't need the noise," he said. "I just want to win."

Steffi Graf played with a quiet intensity that mesmerized the tennis world. Her powerful forehand, often described as a "silencing weapon," cut through opponents like a thunderclap, while her graceful footwork made even the most grueling points seem effortless. She dominated with precision and focus, leaving little room for theatrics. "I never needed the noise," Steffi once said. "The game itself was always enough." That understated demeanor only deepened her mystique as she built one of the most illustrious careers in tennis history.

Born in Mannheim, West Germany, Steffi picked up a racket at the age of three under the guidance of her father, Peter, who coached her in their modest backyard. From the start, her focus was unmatched. She practiced relentlessly, honing every stroke with an almost obsessive drive for perfection. "Tennis wasn't just a sport," she later reflected. "It was my obsession." By 13, she had turned professional, stepping into a world where she would soon rewrite history.

In 1988, Steffi Graf achieved the unimaginable—a feat unmatched in tennis history—winning the "Golden Slam." In a single, electrifying year, she captured all four Grand Slam titles and Olympic gold, sealing her place as the sport's dominant force. And it wasn't just that she won—it was how she won. At Roland Garros, she obliterated Natasha Zvereva 6-0, 6-0 in the final in just 32 minutes, a display of ruthless brilliance. "I didn't think; I just played," Steffi said.

But Steffi's career wasn't defined by one extraordinary season. Over 17 remarkable years, she claimed 22 Grand Slam singles titles, a record that stood for decades as a symbol of greatness. Her versatility set her apart. On the grass courts of Wimbledon, she combined elegance and power to claim seven titles. On the unfor-giving clay of Roland Garros, her relentless precision earned her six trophies. And on the hard courts of the U.S. and Australian Opens, her athleticism and mental stamina made her nearly untouchable.

Steffi's dominance wasn't just about skill; it was her ability to evolve and adapt. Opponents struggled to find weaknesses as she continuously refined her game. "She had no vulnerabilities," one rival said. "Facing her was like facing perfection." For nearly two decades, Steffi transcended the sport, carrying a quiet determination that left no doubt about her greatness.

Her rivalry with Monica Seles brought new emotional intensity to women's tennis. Their gripping battles thrilled fans, but when Seles was tragically stabbed during a match in 1993, Steffi's reaction revealed her character. "It wasn't about tennis anymore," she said. "It was about her well-being." That moment of grace underscored her sportsmanship and compassion.

After retiring in 1999, Steffi married tennis legend Andre Agassi and shifted her focus to family and philanthropy. Through her foundation, Children for Tomorrow, she has tirelessly supported children affected by war and trauma. Steffi brought the same quiet determination and focus that defined her tennis career to her humanitarian work, proving her impact stretched far beyond the court.

Steffi Graf's legacy isn't just about her Golden Slam or 22 Grand Slam titles—it's about how she carried herself. She didn't need fanfare or controversy. She let her game, her discipline and her quiet dominance tell the story. In an era of loud personalities, Steffi proved that true greatness often speaks in whispers.

Kawhi Leonard and Steffi Graf embody leadership through their actions, not their words. Kawhi's key role in the Raptors' championship win highlighted his personal discipline, gaining him broad admiration. Steffi Graf, on the other hand, displayed strategic genius and modesty on the court, setting a high standard for fair play. Both athletes favored personal conduct over personal acclaim, deeply impacting their peers and fans with their understated approaches to leadership. Their stories underscore the power of character, embodied by unpretentiousness, self-awareness and professionalism. Through their emotional intelligence, Leonard and Graf show that leveraging deep personal strengths for the greater good of the team or the sport leads to unity and elevated performance. Their intuitive understanding of teammates and balance in competition showcase leadership's true essence: the power to uplift and inspire.

COURAGE UNDER FIRE: THE BRAVE LEADERSHIP OF JACKIE ROBINSON AND BILLIE JEAN KING

Jackie Robinson's first steps onto a Major League Baseball field in 1947 weren't just the start of an extraordinary career—they were a seismic shift in American history. For over half a century, professional baseball had been segregated, barring black athletes from the game's highest level. That all changed when Brooklyn Dodgers' General Manager Branch Rickey made the bold decision to sign Jackie, breaking the sport's color barrier.

Jackie's journey was marked by determination from an early age. Growing up in Pasadena, California, as the youngest of five children with a single mother, Mallie, who instilled in him the value of dignity and self-respect. At UCLA, Jackie made history as the first to letter in four sports—football, basketball, track and baseball—despite the limited opportunities for black athletes at the time. His undeniable talent eventually led him to the Negro Leagues, playing for the Kansas City Monarchs, where he shone brightly despite the constraints of the era.

In 1945, Branch Rickey summoned Jackie to his office for a meeting that would change history. This wasn't just about baseball—it was about confronting racial injustice on one of America's grandest stages. Rickey needed more than talent; he needed a player with unparalleled courage and composure. Fixing Jackie with a firm gaze, Rickey said, "I'm looking for a player who will not to fight back." Jackie paused and then asked, "Are you looking for a Negro who is afraid to fight back?" Rickey's response was resolute: "No, Robinson. I'm looking for a man with the courage not to." It was clear—Jackie wasn't just being asked to play baseball; he was being asked to carry the hopes of an entire generation.

Jackie's rookie season with the Brooklyn Dodgers in 1947 was a relentless test of his resolve. The racism he faced was brutal. Fans hurled insults and objects. Opponents spiked him deliberately during slides. Even some of his own teammates initially opposed or outright ignored him. Through it all, Jackie refused to break. "I didn't care if they liked me," he said. "All I wanted was for them to respect me."

And respect him they did. Jackie's play spoke louder than the jeers. He hit .297, stole 29 bases and scored 125 runs, earning Rookie of the Year honors. By 1949, Jackie was named the National League MVP, energizing the game with his speed, instincts and fearless style of play. He forced even his harshest critics to acknowledge his brilliance.

One of the most iconic moments of Jackie's career came on September 28, 1955, during Game 1 of the World Series against the New York Yankees. With the Dodgers trailing 6-4, Jackie saw an opening from third base. In a flash, he broke for home plate as Yankees pitcher Whitey Ford delivered. The crowd erupted as Jackie slid headfirst, narrowly beating Yogi Berra's desperate tag. The umpire's "Safe!" call sent the stadium into chaos. Berra furiously argued but Jackie's daring play turned the tide and embodied the tenacity that defined his career. The steal remains one of the most celebrated moments in baseball history.

Jackie's impact extended far beyond the diamond. After retiring in 1956, Jackie continued to use his voice and position. He became a leader in the fight for civil rights, working with the NAACP and supporting political candidates who championed racial justice. His courage on and off the field made him a trailblazer in sports and a leader in the fight for equality. He summed up his mission simply: "A life is not important except in the impact it has on other lives."

Billie Jean King wasn't just a tennis legend—she was a fire-brand, a disruptor, a trailblazer who fought tirelessly for equality. With 39 Grand Slam titles, including 12 singles championships, her fearless approach to the game and unstoppable drive made her a force to be reckoned with. But Billie Jean's legacy extends far beyond trophies—she became a symbol of progress, a champion for gender equality and a leader in redefining women's roles in sports and society.

Her love for tennis began on the public courts of Long Beach, California. At 11 years old, Billie Jean first picked up a racket, quickly standing out not just for her raw talent but her relentless intensity. "Even as a kid I hated losing," she later admitted. Her working-class family supported her passion despite financial struggles. "We couldn't afford tennis whites," she recalled with a smile. "I had to wear my brother's hand-me-downs." That feeling of being an outsider fueled her resolve. By her teenage years, Billie Jean wasn't just a promising player—she was a determined competitor with an unwavering desire to win.

Her success carried her to the pinnacle of tennis but the inequalities she witnessed along the way fueled a deeper purpose. In the 1960s, women in tennis earned a fraction of what their male counterparts took home, no matter their skill or achievements. "We were working just as hard," Billie Jean said, "but we were being treated as less." Never one to stay silent, she began speaking out, demanding equal pay and better opportunities for female athletes. Her voice became a rallying cry for change.

The defining moment of Billie Jean's career—and her fight for equality—came in 1973 with the legendary *"Battle of the Sexes."* Bobby Riggs, a former men's champion and self-proclaimed chauvinist, publicly ridiculed women's tennis, claiming no woman could beat him, even at the age of 55. He mocked Billie Jean as "the leader of the women's liberation army," calling her talent overrated. For Billie Jean, this wasn't just about tennis—it was a fight for respect.

On September 20, 1973, in front of 90 million viewers worldwide, Billie Jean stepped onto the court at the Houston Astrodome with the weight of a movement on her shoulders. "If I lost," she later said, "it would set women's progress back 50 years." Riggs relied on theatrics and trash talk to rattle her, but Billie Jean remained laser-focused. With precision and supreme fitness, she dismantled him. Riggs struggled to keep up as Billie Jean dictated the pace, winning in straight sets—6-4, 6-3, 6-3.

When the final point was won, Billie Jean lifted her arms high, victorious not just for herself but for women everywhere. "It wasn't just a win," she said. "It was a statement." That moment shifted the conversation around gender equality, proving women belonged on center stage.

Billie Jean didn't stop there. That same year, she founded the Women's Tennis Association (WTA) and secured equal prize money at the U.S. Open, making it the first Grand Slam to do so. Her actions inspired similar movements in other sports, paving the way for future generations of female athletes.

Off the court, Billie Jean remained just as courageous. As one of the first high-profile athletes to advocate for LGBTQ+ rights, she faced immense scrutiny but stood firm. "To be yourself in a world that tells you to be someone else is the greatest act of bravery," she said.

Jackie Robinson and Billie Jean King emerged as leaders by challenging the status quo and championing equality. Robinson's dignified resilience against racial hostility in Major League Baseball and King's vocal advocacy for gender equality in tennis marked them as pioneers who transcended their sports to create societal change. Their actions underscored a commitment to justice, showcasing a pillar of leadership: the courage to stand firm for one's beliefs amidst adversity. Supported by mentors like Dodgers' GM

Branch Rickey for Robinson and influential coaches and peers for King, both athletes demonstrated the power of integrity, perseverance and emotional intelligence. Their blend of humility and assertiveness earned widespread respect. Through their stories, we learn that true leadership is about inspiring change and empowering others, proving that by embracing our authentic selves, we can leave a lasting impact on society.

INTERCONNECTING THE STORIES OF LEADERSHIP AND CHARACTER BUILDING OF THE SIX ATHLETES

Through the narratives of LeBron James, Abby Wambach, Kawhi Leonard, Steffi Graf, Jackie Robinson and Billie Jean King, some unified leadership themes emerge: personal resolve, integrity, authenticity, emotional intelligence and the readiness to inspire others. Most of these athletes, while achieving greatness in their respective sports, have meaningfully impacted society by embodying various leadership styles and facing challenges head-on. LeBron and Abby extend their influence beyond their sports, using their platforms for community betterment and gender equality. Their actions underscore that leadership grounds itself on and then transcends personal achievements—it's about advocating for change and lifting others. Kawhi and Steffi, on the other hand, demonstrate leadership through humility and silent perseverance. Their journey teaches us the power of leading by example and the respect and legacy that such an approach can cultivate. Jackie Robinson and Billie Jean King tackled societal barriers bravely and gracefully, challenging racial and gender inequalities. Their stories prove that leadership often requires confronting injustice, even in adversity; in fact, usually in adversity. By intertwining these athletes' stories, we see leadership as a diverse and dynamic concept shaped by personal values and the courage to make impactful choices.

————

REFLECTION QUESTIONS:

• *Personal Values in Leadership:* Think about the causes or values you feel most passionate about. Are there moments when you've stood up for something or supported someone in need? How do your values align with the actions of LeBron James, Abby Wambach or Billie Jean King?

• *Leading by Example:* Kawhi Leonard and Steffi Graf led quietly but powerfully. Think about times when you may have felt inspired by someone quiet but strong and principled. Reflect on some times when your own actions spoke louder than words. What did you observe in how this may have influenced others? What did you learn about the impact of humility and consistency?

• *Facing Injustice:* Jackie Robinson's courage in confronting racism and Billie Jean King's fight for gender equality demonstrate leadership in the face of adversity. Have you ever encountered a situation where you needed to stand up for yourself or someone else? How did you handle it and what could you do differently next time?

• *Your Leadership Style:* Leadership takes many forms, from loud advocacy to quiet action. What type of leadership feels natural to you? Are you a motivator like Abby, a strategist like Kawhi or a change-maker like Jackie? How might you grow your leadership skills while staying authentic to yourself?

Take a few minutes to write down your thoughts, focusing on what leadership means to you and how you'd like to embody it in your life.

. . .

Action Plan: Becoming the Leader You Aspire to Be

• *Define Your Leadership Identity:* Choose three words that represent the kind of leader you want to be (e.g., courageous, compassionate, persistent). Write them down and reflect on how you can embody these qualities daily. Keep these words visible in a journal, on your mirror or as a phone wallpaper to remind yourself of your aspirations.

• *Advocate for a Cause:* Identify a cause or issue you care about. It could be as big as promoting environmental awareness or as personal as standing up for a friend who needs help. Take one small step this week to support that cause, such as raising awareness on social media, joining a club or volunteering.

• *Lead by Quiet Example:* Think of one area where your actions can inspire others without needing many words. This could be working hard on a group project, being the first to apologize in a conflict or consistently showing kindness to those around you. Pay attention to how others respond and how it feels to influence through action rather than speech.

• *Challenge Yourself:* Leadership often means stepping out of your comfort zone. This week, set a goal to do something that stretches your confidence—whether it's speaking up in class, trying out for a new role or starting a conversation with someone who might need a friend.

• *Learn from Role Models:* Choose one athlete from this chapter whose leadership story resonates most with you. Research more about their life and challenges. What specific traits or decisions made them successful leaders? Write down one thing you can emulate in your own journey.

• *Build a Support Network:* Leadership doesn't happen in isolation. Surround yourself with people who share your values and inspire you to grow. Consider asking a teacher, coach or family member for advice or feedback on improving as a leader.

• *Celebrate Small Wins:* Leadership is a journey not a destination. Each time you advocate for a cause, help someone in need or take a brave step, recognize it as progress. Begin a "leadership chapter" in your journal" to record these moments, reminding yourself of the growth you're achieving.

Remember, leadership is not about being the loudest or most visible—it's about making authentic choices, standing up for your beliefs and inspiring others through your actions. Whether you lead through bold advocacy or quiet perseverance, your journey matters. Reflect, take action and trust that every step forward brings you closer to becoming the leader you're meant to be.

In the next chapter, we'll explore the power of mental toughness and how athletes overcome self-doubt to achieve greatness and become leaders. This builds on the themes of resilience and developing character and offers new insights into the mindset required to face challenges head-on.

4 MENTAL TOUGHNESS

THE MIND GAME: MICHAEL JORDAN AND MARTINA NAVRATILOVA'S MENTAL MASTERY

IMAGINE STANDING at the free-throw line, the arena roaring with anticipation, the game clock dwindling and the weight of an entire team resting on your shoulders. For Michael Jordan, this wasn't just a moment—it was destiny. Few athletes in history have captured the world's imagination like Jordan, a name synonymous with greatness, mental toughness and unrelenting drive. But his rise to the pinnacle of basketball was anything but smooth; it was a saga of steel, setbacks and iconic triumphs.

Michael's journey began humbly in Wilmington, North Carolina. He spent endless hours shooting hoops in his backyard as a boy, fueled by dreams of making it big. But in 10th grade, the unthinkable happened—he was cut from his high school varsity team. Heartbroken but resolute, Michael turned failure into fuel. "It made me work harder than I ever had," he later said. Day after day, he practiced obsessively, sharpening his skills and turning rejection into the foundation of his fire. By senior year, he wasn't just on the team—he was its star, capturing the attention of college scouts.

At the University of North Carolina, Michael's legend ignited. As a freshman in the 1982 NCAA Championship, with the game on the line, the ball found its way into his hands. Calm and collected, he elevated and drained the game-winning shot. That moment—clutch, confident and unforgettable—galvanized his belief in himself. "That shot," he later said, "gave me the confidence to succeed under pressure." It was a foreshadowing of the countless heart-stopping moments that would follow.

Drafted third overall by the Chicago Bulls in 1984, Michael wasted no time transforming the franchise. His high-flying dunks and jaw-dropping athleticism earned him the nickname "Air Jordan," making the Bulls must-watch basketball. But what set him apart wasn't just his highlight reels—it was his mindset. "I can accept failure but I can't accept not trying," he said. That relentless drive pushed him past limits, inspiring teammates and leaving opponents scrambling to keep up.

Michael's work ethic was legendary. Former Bulls coach Phil Jackson recalled, "He wasn't just the hardest worker—he demanded everyone rise to his level." Teammates spoke of grueling early morning workouts, where Michael's pursuit of perfection set an unrelenting standard. He didn't just play to win—he played to dominate.

The defining stretch of his career came in the 1990s, a reign of dominance that saw the Bulls capture six NBA championships, including two historic three-peats (1991–1993, 1996–1998). Each title told a story of grit, leadership and the sheer will to win, but the 1997 *"Flu Game"* became the stuff of legend.

It was Game 5 of the NBA Finals against the Utah Jazz and Michael fell violently ill, weakened by a fever of 103 degrees. Looking visibly drained, he still took the court, refusing to let his team down. What followed defied belief: 38 points, including a critical three-pointer in the final minutes. When the buzzer sounded, he collapsed into Scottie Pippen's arms, completely spent. "Giving up wasn't an option," Michael said. That night, his greatness wasn't defined by talent alone but by his refusal to let adversity win.

Off the court, Michael's influence stretched far beyond basketball. His partnership with Nike and the birth of the Air Jordan brand revolutionized sports marketing, turning him into a global icon. But his story of resilience and unshakable self-belief transcended sport, inspiring athletes and dreamers alike. "Some people want it to happen, some wish it would happen, others make it happen," he once said.

Martina Navratilova: tennis legend, transformative figure and trailblazer. With 18 Grand Slam singles titles and a staggering 59 major titles, Martina's dominance on the court was undeniable. But her journey was anything but straightforward—it was forged through personal loss, bold decisions and an unyielding desire to excel.

Martina grew up behind the Iron Curtain in communist Czechoslovakia. Her ski instructor father instilled in her a deep sense of drive and determination. But when Martina was just eight years old, tragedy struck—her father's sudden death left her reeling. Tennis became her refuge. "On the court," she said, "I felt free. It was where I could be myself." Determined to make something of her life, Martina poured herself into the game, rising through the ranks of the local tennis circuit.

By her teens, Martina's extraordinary talent had caught the world's attention. But as a citizen of a tightly controlled communist regime, she faced harsh barriers. Competing on the international stage was a distant dream; freedom itself felt unattainable. At just 18, Martina made the agonizing decision to defect to the United States, leaving behind her family and homeland. "I didn't know if I'd ever see them again," she admitted. "But I couldn't let fear stop me." With a small suitcase and an enormous leap of faith, Martina boarded the plane, heart pounding but resolve unwavering.

Her professional start in the United States wasn't easy. Martina's raw talent dazzled but lacked consistency. Her aggressive serve-and-volley game was electric, yet she struggled with fitness and mental focus. Often in the shadow of her cool, methodical rival Chris Evert, Martina grew frustrated. That all changed after a pivotal conversation with Billie Jean King. "She told me, 'It's not the losses that define you. It's what you do next,'" Martina recalled. Inspired, she embraced a total transformation.

She took apart and reassembled her game, becoming the first female tennis player to focus on fitness and nutrition with cutting-edge intensity. Unheard of in women's tennis at the time, weight training turned Martina into a physical powerhouse. By the early 1980s, Martina had evolved into a near-perfect athlete—strong, fast and tactically brilliant. Her left-handed serve became a weapon, her volleys razor-sharp. Suddenly, her rivalry with Chris Evert—Evert's calm baseline play versus Martina's fearless attacks at the net—produced some of the most electrifying matches in tennis history. Martina ultimately dominated, winning 13 of their final 15 Grand Slam encounters, etching her name into the records of the sport's greatest rivalries.

Off the court, Martina's courage was just as impactful. One of the first openly gay athletes in professional sports, she came out in the 1980s, defying immense backlash. "I wasn't going to hide who I was," she declared. At a time when LGBTQ+ representation in sports was nearly nonexistent, Martina's boldness made her a trailblazer, inspiring countless others to embrace their authentic selves.

Her influence stretched far beyond her playing career. Even in retirement, Martina remained a force—a mentor, a commentator and a champion for equality. She continued to break boundaries, capturing her final Grand Slam title at age 49 in mixed doubles, a testament to her competitive fire and longevity. Her legacy—a blend of athletic brilliance, mental fortitude and fearless authenticity—proves that greatness is about far more than trophies.

Both Michael Jordan and Martina Navratilova showcased unparalleled mental toughness, using psychological tactics and self-discipline to excel under pressure. Michael's mindset of viewing setbacks as opportunities and Martina's willpower to change course and tackle demanding physical conditioning enabled them to use challenges as stepping stones for success. Their resilience, mindsets and meticulous mental preparation were key to their legendary status in sports.

OVERCOMING DOUBT: THE MENTAL BATTLES OF NOVAK DJOKOVIC AND ALLYSON FELIX

Novak Djokovic, now a titan of tennis with 24 Grand Slam titles (as of 2024), wasn't always seen as destined for greatness. Although his early career showed flashes of brilliance, inconsistency, injuries and self-doubt often dimmed his promise. Emerging in an era dominated by Roger Federer and Rafael Nadal —two of tennis's most celebrated icons—Novak seemed perpetually in their shadow. Critics praised his talent but questioned his physical and mental endurance to break into their elite tier.

Novak's journey began in war-torn Serbia, where adversity shaped his resilience. As a child, he practiced on makeshift courts carved into mountain roads near his modest home. "There were moments we trained through air-raid sirens," he recalled. "The war taught me to fight for every point, every chance." The backdrop of bomb shelters and uncertainty forged an unshakable toughness that would later define his career.

By 2008, Novak made his breakthrough with his first Grand

Slam title at the Australian Open, signaling his arrival as a legitimate contender. But the years that followed were grueling. Frequent retirements, fatigue and erratic results left him chasing Federer and Nadal. "It wasn't just my body—it was my mind," he admitted. Determined to rise above, Novak overhauled his lifestyle. He adopted a strict gluten-free diet after discovering an intolerance, revamped his fitness regimen to build stamina and incorporated meditation and visualization techniques to sharpen his mental edge. "I had to learn how to silence the noise in my head," he said.

Everything clicked in 2011, the year Novak transformed into an unstoppable force. He captured three Grand Slam titles, went on a 41-match winning streak and repeatedly bested Nadal and Federer. His game had evolved—his defensive skills were impenetrable, his precision unmatched. But more importantly, his belief had solidified. "I realized I could beat anyone in any moment," he said.

This mental fortitude reached its zenith in the 2019 Wimbledon final, one of the greatest matches in tennis history. Facing Federer, the crowd favorite, Novak battled more than just his rival—he fought against the weight of history and a stadium full of voices rooting for his defeat. Down two championship points in the fifth set, the title appeared to belong to Federer. Yet Novak refused to yield. Gritting through pressure that would have broken many, he clawed back into the match, responding to Federer's brilliance with calm, calculated resilience.

The final, stretching nearly five hours, became the longest in Wimbledon history. The tension was palpable, every point a battle unto itself. The crowd roared with every Federer success but Novak remained composed. "When they chanted 'Roger,' I heard 'Novak,'" he quipped afterward, masking the immense psychological strength it took to withstand the moment. When the final point fell in his favor, Novak collapsed onto the grass, arms wide, a mix of relief and triumph. It wasn't just a win—it was a testament to his unyielding determination.

Novak's journey from underdog to legend is as much about mindset as it is about skill. Open about his battles with self-doubt and immense pressure, he redefined how mental strength shapes success. "Mental training is as important as physical," he said. "It's about belief, resilience and pushing through when everything feels impossible."

Allyson Felix's journey to becoming one of the greatest track and field athletes of all time is as much about grit and transformation as it is about her dazzling speed and record-breaking performances. A six-time Olympian with 13 World Championship titles, Felix combined physical brilliance with unyielding mental resilience. But the woman on the podium was far more than a champion; she was someone who had overcome challenges that tested her in every way.

Growing up in Los Angeles, Allyson's talent was clear early on. With blazing speed and relentless determination, she dominated high school meets and caught the attention of college recruiters and professional scouts. At just 18, Allyson burst onto the global stage at the 2004 Athens Olympics. Stepping into the 200m final against the world's fastest sprinters, she carried nerves, grit and absolute conviction. Surging ahead, she claimed silver—a remarkable feat for a teenager. "That race showed me I belonged," she later said. But for Felix, second wasn't enough. "I didn't just want to compete—I wanted to be the best."

Four years later, she earned her first Olympic gold as part of the dominant U.S. 4x400m relay team. Yet, the 200m gold remained elusive. In 2012, at the London Olympics, Felix returned with quiet resolve. When the gun fired, she exploded out of the blocks with a flawless stride, crossing the finish line in a stunning 21.88 seconds to claim gold. Tears of joy followed. "It wasn't just about winning," she said. "It was about everything I overcame to get here." That victory made certain of her legacy and proved that perseverance can achieve the impossible.

The Rio 2016 Olympics brought another defining moment. In the dramatic 400m final, Felix powered down the home stretch, only to be edged out by a diving finish. Silver was hers, but disappointment didn't hold her back. Days later, she anchored the U.S. 4x100m and 4x400m relay teams, delivering flawless runs to secure two more gold medals.

In 2018, Allyson's greatest test came off the track. While pregnant with her daughter, she was diagnosed with preeclampsia, a life-threatening condition. Camryn was delivered prematurely via an emergency C-section. The experience transformed her perspective. "Everything I thought was important shifted," she said. Determined to fight for maternal health, Felix began using her platform to advocate for women facing similar struggles.

In 2019, her advocacy grew louder. When Nike, her longtime sponsor, attempted to cut her pay during her pregnancy, Allyson spoke out. In a powerful op-ed, she called out systemic inequities, exposing how motherhood is treated as a liability in sports. "I couldn't stand by and let this happen—not to me or to the women who would come after me." Her courage ignited global conversations about gender equality, forcing Nike to revise its policies and protect pregnant athletes.

Defying all odds, Allyson returned for the Tokyo 2020 Olympics (held in 2021). Competing as both a mother and an advocate, she claimed bronze in the 400m and gold in the 4x400m relay. Her total of 11 Olympic medals—7 gold, 3 silver, and 1 bronze—made her the most decorated female track and field Olympian in history.

Novak Djokovic and Allyson Felix epitomize the essence of focus, demonstrating how mental fortitude propels extraordinary achievement. Djokovic's journey from uncertainty to tennis supremacy exemplifies the virtues of growth and adaptability. In contrast, Felix's remarkable longevity as a track and field athlete, plus as an advocate for athletes' health and rights, underscore her resilience and commitment to societal change. Their dedication to mental fitness enhances their legacy, with Djokovic's mindfulness practices and Felix's durability and comprehensive approach to well-being in sports. Although employing different methods— Djokovic, through deliberate mental conditioning, and Felix, through her endurance and advocacy for equality—show the diverse paths to cultivating and relying on mental strength. Their experiences reveal the golden nugget inside adversity: its power to teach and transform.

CONQUERING FEAR: THE MENTAL RESILIENCE OF LINDSEY HORAN AND SHAUN WHITE

Lindsey Horan has carved out a reputation as a dominant force in women's soccer, blending technical brilliance with unyielding mental resilience. Her journey is marked by bold choices, fierce determination and a refusal to follow convention—beginning with a decision that shocked the soccer world. At just 18, Lindsey became the first American woman to forgo college soccer, signing with Paris Saint-Germain (PSG). "I wanted to challenge myself in every possible way," she said. That leap of faith set her on a unique trajectory, showcasing her courage and relentless drive to compete at the highest levels.

The move to Paris was anything but easy. Lindsey was far from home, immersed in an unfamiliar culture and facing the unrelenting demands of European soccer. The pace of play was faster, the technical expectations sharper and the pressure to perform constant. "It felt like being thrown into the deep end," she later admitted. She had to refine her ball control, sharpen her decision-making and master tactical nuances. But beyond the physical challenges, it was the mental strain—the loneliness, the self-doubt—that tested her resolve the most.

Lindsey turned to mindfulness to cope, a practice that would become a cornerstone of her success. Amid grueling training sessions and high-pressure matches, she found calm through grounding techniques like deep breathing and visualization. "I'd close my eyes and picture myself in control—calm, confident and focused," she explained. Before every game, she centered herself, blocking out distractions and mentally rehearsing her responses to difficult situations on the field. This preparation became her lifeline, allowing her to quiet doubt and focus on the present moment.

The results spoke for themselves. Mindfulness gave Lindsey a critical edge, helping her remain composed under pressure—whether threading a perfect pass, winning a duel or recovering from mistakes. "Instead of letting errors weigh me down, I learned to let them go and move on," she said. This mental discipline and her relentless work ethic transformed her into a rising star at PSG.

When Lindsey returned to the U.S. Women's National Team (USWNT), she was no longer just a promising talent—she was a seasoned competitor. Her ability to quickly dictate the tempo, deliver pinpoint passes and excel in clutch moments made her indispensable. Whether playing as a midfielder or stepping up as an attacking threat, her versatility and tactical intelligence became hallmarks of her game.

Her defining moment came during the FIFA Women's World Cup, where Lindsey delivered when her team needed her most. In a pivotal match, she soared for a header in the box, driving the ball past the goalkeeper with precision—a goal that locked in her reputation as a player who thrives under pressure. "In those moments, I remind myself to stay present," she said. That calm, developed through her Paris experience, became her secret weapon on soccer's biggest stage.

Off the field, Lindsey has become a leading voice for mental health. She shares her struggles with performance anxiety and the tools that helped her overcome them. From mindfulness techniques to speaking openly about asking for help, she encourages others to confront their fears. "It's okay not to have it all together," she says. Strength comes from facing what scares you most." Her vulnerability has resonated globally, helping to break down stigmas and inspire athletes to prioritize their well-being.

Shaun White is a snowboarding legend and an epic symbol of daring, focus and reinvention. His journey is one of incredible heights, devastating falls and mental toughness that pushed him to redefine his sport. With his fiery red hair and jaw-dropping tricks, the "Flying Tomato" captivated the world. But behind the gold medals and roaring crowds lies a story forged in fearlessness and tenacity.

Shaun's love for snowboarding began on the slopes of Big Bear Mountain Resort in Southern California. Family trips from their home in San Diego became the backdrop of his childhood. Born with a congenital heart defect, Shaun underwent two major surgeries before the age of five. "I still have the scars," he said. "They remind me of what I've overcome." By six, he was already tearing down mountains with fearless determination, carving through snow with a focus far beyond his years.

By his teens, Shaun had become a prodigy, dazzling audiences with audacious tricks and unmatched style. But the pressure to perform at the top was relentless. "Every competition felt like the world was watching," he admitted. That pressure reached a breaking point in 2017 during a training session in New Zealand. Attempting a double cork 1440, he launched into the air, twisting and spinning. But he over-rotated and slammed face-first into the lip of the halfpipe.

Blood spread into the snow as Shaun lay motionless. "I thought, 'This might be it,'" he later confessed. His team rushed to his side and he was taken to the hospital for 62 stitches across his face. The physical scars were one thing but the mental toll was far greater.

Recovery was brutal. "I had to start from scratch," Shaun admitted, the crash etched into his memory. But instead of retreating, he turned to visualization and meditation to face his fear head-on. He replayed the crash in his mind—studying it, learning from it. "I visualized every detail—the height, the rotation, the moment it went wrong. I had to understand it to overcome it," he explained.

Meditation anchored him, quieting the doubts that threatened to consume him. Shaun rebuilt himself in his mind and in practice, one small victory at a time: a clean jump, a trick performed without hesitation, a perfect carve. Each success chipped away at the fear. "It wasn't just about getting back on the board—it was about proving to myself that I still had it," he said.

His ultimate test came at the 2018 Winter Olympics in PyeongChang. Critics doubted whether he could reclaim his dominance. In the men's halfpipe final, Shaun stood atop the pipe for his final run, sitting in second place. The stakes couldn't have been higher. "I told myself, 'You've been here before. You know what to do.'"

As he launched into the run, time seemed to slow. Each trick —frontside 1440, back-to-back 1260s and his signature Double McTwist 1260—was flawless. When the score—97.75—flashed on the screen, Shaun dropped to his knees, tears streaming down his face. "That run wasn't just for the medal," he said. "It was for every doubt I overcame, every time I picked myself up."

Lindsey Horan and Shaun White demonstrate how fear can catalyze growth. Horan's performance under pressure, rooted in mindfulness and illustrating mental resilience, makes her a fine role model for young athletes. Similarly, White's openness about his mental health challenges after his shocking accident underscores the importance of addressing such issues head-on. Despite differing obstacles—Horan's anxiety and White's recovery from his injuries—their commitment to self-awareness and mental discipline shines through. Their approaches, from Horan's meditations to White's visualizations, show that mental toughness takes different forms, transforming vulnerability into strength.

INTERCONNECTING THE STORIES OF MENTAL TOUGHNESS OF THE SIX ATHLETES

Reflecting on the stories of Michael Jordan, Martina Navratilova, Novak Djokovic, Allyson Felix, Lindsey Horan and Shaun White, a unified theme of mental toughness emerges as the cornerstone of their success. This quality isn't about sheer strength or speed; it's about the tenacity found within, the ability to persevere through adversity and the capacity for self-improvement in the face of challenges. Michael and Martina exemplify how to handle the pressures of being elite athletes, employing visualization and mindfulness to maintain focus and mental clarity amid high expectations. Similarly, Novak and Allyson's stories of overcoming self-doubt and criticism through positive affirmations and celebrating small victories teach us the importance of self-belief and motivation derived from imposed limitations. Lindsey and Shaun's experiences add another dimension, illustrating the necessity of confronting fear and anxiety directly. Their success showcases how mental resilience, bolstered by mindfulness, meditation and a methodical return to form, can transform fear into triumph, such as in Lindsey's elite play and Shaun's gold medal performances. These athletes' stories collectively underscore that mental toughness shows up in various forms, rooted in individual experiences and challenges. Whether it's Michael's determination, Martina's self-improvement, Novak's self-belief, Allyson's advocacy,

Lindsey's pressure management or Shaun's recovery and fear confrontation, each narrative provides unique insights into developing mental strength.

———

REFLECTION: UNDERSTANDING YOUR INNER STRENGTH

Mental toughness is not about being immune to fear, pressure or self-doubt; it's about how you respond to those challenges. Each athlete in this chapter has shown that mental strength is a skill that can be developed. It is not an innate quality only reserved for the extraordinary. Find some quiet time, pick up your journal and reflect on the following questions to explore your own mental resilience:

• *Handling Pressure:* Michael Jordan and Martina Navratilova used techniques like visualization and meditation to stay focused. Think about a time when you felt overwhelmed by pressure. What methods, if any, did you use to manage it? Could visualization or mindfulness help you in future situations?

• *Turning Criticism into Fuel:* Novak Djokovic and Allyson Felix faced external doubts and internal struggles but transformed them into motivation. How do you currently handle criticism or setbacks? Do you let them define you or use them as opportunities for growth? How can you reframe criticism in your own head to strengthen your resolve?

• *Confronting Fear:* Lindsey Horan and Shaun White didn't shy away from fear; they leaned into it, using their experiences to grow stronger. Is there a fear or anxiety holding you back? Challenge yourself to write about it in the private space of your journal. How might confronting it directly, as these athletes did, help you overcome it?

• *Your Resilience Journey:* Mental toughness is built through experience, practice and reflection. What current challenge are you facing that could be an opportunity to develop greater mental resilience? What small steps can you take to build your confidence and mental strength? Jot down your thoughts to clarify how you can apply these lessons in your own life.

ACTION PLAN: BUILDING MENTAL TOUGHNESS INTO YOUR STORY

• *Practice Visualization:* Take five minutes daily to visualize yourself succeeding in a goal or overcoming a challenge. Picture every detail—how you feel, what you see and the steps you take to get there. Visualization, like Michael Jordan's or Shaun White's, can help you build confidence and focus.

• *Use Positive Affirmations:* Write down three affirmations that resonate with you, such as "I am capable of overcoming challenges" or "Setbacks are growth opportunities." Repeat them daily, especially during difficult moments, as Novak Djokovic and Allyson Felix did.

• *Celebrate Small Wins:* Break down a current challenge into smaller, manageable goals. Celebrate each step you accomplish, no matter how small. Recognizing progress builds confidence and reminds you that growth happens incrementally.

• *Face Your Fears:* Identify one fear or anxiety that's been holding you back. It could be speaking in front of others, trying out for a team or taking a tough exam. Plan one small step to confront it this week, inspired by Lindsey Horan and Shaun White's courage.

• *Develop a Mindfulness Habit:* Dedicate five to ten minutes daily to mindfulness or meditation. Focus on your breath, let go of distractions and ground yourself in the present moment. This practice can help you build clarity and calm under pressure, just as Martina did.

• *Reframe Setbacks:* The next time you encounter a failure or setback, pause and reflect. Ask yourself: What can I learn from this? How can this experience make me stronger? Write down your insights to remind yourself that setbacks are steps toward growth.

• *Build a Resilience Toolbox:* Create a "mental toughness toolkit" with strategies that work for you. This could include deep breathing exercises, journaling, reaching out to a mentor or listening to a motivational song. Experiment with different techniques to discover what helps you stay mentally strong.

• *Share Your Journey:* Talk about mental toughness with a friend, family member, coach or teammate. Share what you've learned from this chapter and discuss strategies you can practice together. Supporting others and being supported in return strengthens resilience.

Remember, mental toughness isn't about being perfect or invulnerable. It's about showing up, even when it's hard and taking steps toward your goals—no matter how small. Just like these athletes, you have the power to cultivate mental strength through deliberate practice, self-reflection and courage. Embrace the journey and trust that with each challenge you face, you're becoming more potent, more resilient and better equipped to handle whatever comes your way.

TIME OUT

"It's not about the number of points you score. It's about how you make the people around you better."
– Steve Nash, all-time great NBA point guard.

Dear Reader,

Thank you for reading *Game Changers: Inspirational Sports Stories*. I hope these stories have inspired you so far and offered new insights on resilience, character and the power of sports to shape lives.

If you feel this book has positively impacted you, perhaps you, yourself, can step into the role model spot. You can help others by writing a thoughtful review of this book. Many young people like you are searching for direction and inspiration; a review is by far the best way to help them discover this book.

Your review doesn't have to be long—it takes just a couple of minutes and is free.

Book reviews are one of the top ways people decide which book to buy. If this book has inspired or empowered you, your words could do the same for someone else.

Take a moment now to share your thoughts while the stories are fresh. For **e-book readers**, you can click on the link below and you will be taken directly to Amazon's review page for the book. For **printed version readers**, you can use the photo app on your phone to scan the QR code below which will also take you directly to the same review page. It takes just a moment to rate the book and add your thoughts.

Your review can do more than describe the book—it can encourage someone to start their own journey toward self-confidence, personal growth and leadership. By writing a review, you're becoming part of the mission to inspire others. Your words can help someone believe in their potential, overcome challenges and take charge of their own path—just as this book has inspired you.

Thank you for helping me share these stories. Together, we can inspire even more people to become Game Changers in their own lives.

Review link coming soon.

QR code coming soon.

5 DIVERSITY AND BREAKING BARRIERS

BREAKING BOUNDARIES: THE TRAILBLAZING PATHS OF MUHAMMAD ALI AND ROBERTO CLEMENTE

MUHAMMAD ALI WASN'T JUST a boxing legend—he was a symbol of defiance, courage and transformation. Born Cassius Clay in 1942 in Louisville, Kentucky, Ali grew up in a segregated world that sought to limit his potential. At 12 years old, his life changed when his beloved bicycle was stolen. Furious, he stormed into a local gym, shouting, "I'm gonna whip whoever took my bike!" The trainer, Joe Martin, handed him gloves and cautioned, "If you're gonna fight, you'd better learn how to do it right."

Ali's passion for boxing grew as he trained relentlessly, turning frustration into discipline. From the very start, he was extraordinary. In the ring, he moved like a dancer—light on his feet and impossible to predict. His speed, precision and mental edge set him apart. "Float like a butterfly, sting like a bee," he'd rhyme, turning every fight into a spectacle. Fans couldn't get enough of his confidence. "I am the greatest!" he proclaimed before ever winning a title, and soon the world believed him.

In 1964, at just 22, Ali stepped into the ring against the feared Sonny Liston. The odds were stacked against the brash challenger, but Ali predicted victory. "I'm gonna shock the world," he said. Dancing around Liston, he unleashed a flurry of lightning-fast punches, dismantling the heavyweight champion in seven rounds. When it was over, Ali stood triumphant, fists raised, shouting, "I'm the king of the world!"

But his fight extended beyond the ring. Days later, Ali made headlines again by announcing his conversion to Islam and rejecting the name Cassius Clay, calling it "a slave name." "I am Muhammad Ali—a free man," he declared, boldly tying his identity to the fight for racial equality.

Ali's courage knew no limits. In 1967, at the height of his career, he refused to be drafted into the Vietnam War, citing his faith and opposition to the conflict. "I ain't got no quarrel with them Viet Cong," he said. The backlash was swift: Ali was stripped of his titles, banned from boxing and faced the threat of prison. Yet, he stood firm. "I'm standing up for my beliefs," he said. "If it means facing a firing squad, so be it."

Ali's return to the ring in 1970 began his legendary second act, which was defined by historic clashes. His trilogy with Joe Frazier, including the brutal "Thrilla in Manila," showcased his resilience. But it was the 1974 "Rumble in the Jungle" against the undefeated George Foreman that ensured his status as "The Greatest."

Foreman, a powerhouse, was expected to demolish Ali. Instead, Ali shocked the world with his "rope-a-dope" strategy—leaning on the ropes and absorbing Foreman's furious punches, taunting him between rounds: "Is that all you got, George? Is that all you got?" As Foreman tired, Ali struck. Ali unleashed a perfect combination in the eighth round, flooring Foreman and reclaiming his crown. The crowd erupted as Ali raised his arms in triumph. "I told you I was the greatest!"

Even as Parkinson's disease slowed his body in later years, Ali's spirit remained unshaken. His lighting of the Olympic torch in 1996 brought the world to tears, a testament to his enduring impact. "Service to others is the rent you pay for your room here on earth," he said—a belief he lived until his passing in 2016.

Roberto Clemente wasn't just a baseball legend—he was a symbol of resilience, pride and selfless humanity. Born in 1934 in Carolina, Puerto Rico, Clemente grew up with a burning passion for baseball. His first "bat" was a guava tree branch, his first "field" a dusty patch of dirt. "I always knew I wanted to play baseball," he said, recalling how he'd practice barefoot under the Puerto Rican sun, tirelessly perfecting the swing that would one day make history.

Clemente's road to Major League Baseball wasn't as smooth as his graceful throws from right field. In 1955, at just 20 years old, he joined the Pittsburgh Pirates in a league dominated by white, English-speaking players. He faced relentless barriers: his name was mispronounced, his accent mocked and his abilities questioned. Reporters tried anglicizing him as "Bobby," but Clemente stood firm. "I'm not a 'Bobby,'" he said. "I don't believe in color. I believe in people."

On the field, Clemente was poetry in motion. His legendary throwing arm was unparalleled—it's said he could start with his back foot against the outfield wall and fire a perfect strike to home plate, the ball never rising more than 15 feet. Baserunners advanced at their own peril. His bat was just as dangerous, earning him a career .317 batting average and exactly 3,000 hits, a milestone he reached in his final at-bat in 1972. Yet, it was Clemente's passion and style of play that truly set him apart. "I don't just play baseball," he once said. "I give everything I have."

Clemente's defining moment came in the 1971 World Series

against the heavily favored Baltimore Orioles. At 37 years old, he played like a man possessed, batting an extraordinary .414 and delivering defensive gems that stunned even his opponents. In Game 7, with the championship hanging in the balance, Clemente stepped to the plate, the weight of his team—and his heritage—on his shoulders. With a calm intensity, he launched a clutch double down the right-field line, shifting momentum and helping the Pirates clinch the title.

Named Series MVP, Clemente later reflected, "I wanted to show the world that a Latin player could be just as great as anyone else." And he did. For millions in Puerto Rico and across Latin America, Clemente's triumph was more than a victory—it was proof that talent and determination could break barriers and redefine possibilities.

Off the field, Clemente fought just as hard. He became a fierce advocate for Latin American players, calling out discrimination and misrepresentation. Proud of his Puerto Rican roots, he used his platform to help others, organizing baseball clinics for underprivileged kids and delivering aid to communities in need. "I want to be remembered as a man who gave all he had to give," Clemente said, words he embodied daily.

Tragically, on New Year's Eve in 1972, Clemente's life was cut short when his plane crashed en route to Nicaragua, where he was delivering supplies to earthquake victims. He was just 38 years old. The loss sent shockwaves through the world but his legacy only grew stronger.

In 1973, Clemente became the first Latin American inducted into the Baseball Hall of Fame, bypassing the customary five-year waiting period. Today, the Roberto Clemente Award honors MLB players who exemplify his spirit of sportsmanship and humanitarianism.

Muhammad Ali and Roberto Clemente transcended their roles as athletes to become symbols of social justice, each advocating passionately for causes dear to them. Ali, with his resolute opposition to the Vietnam War based on his religious convictions and moral principles, faced the forfeiture of his titles but solidified his legacy as a civil rights champion. Clemente, meanwhile, used his prominence to challenge racial prejudice and the exclusion of Latin American players in baseball, promoting inclusivity and pioneering athlete-led social initiatives. Both faced daunting obstacles—Ali contending with racial discrimination and Clemente combating Latin stereotypes and xenophobia—yet neither wavered in their dedication to using their platforms to drive positive social impact. Ali's celebrated return to boxing and Clemente's unwavering humanitarian efforts highlight how personal success can be a powerful vehicle for societal uplift.

CHAMPIONS OF CHANGE: HOW MEGAN RAPINOE AND ANTHONY JOSHUA INSPIRE EQUALITY AND OPPORTUNITY

Megan Rapinoe's journey to becoming a global icon began in Redding, California, where she and her twin sister, Rachael, spent countless hours playing backyard soccer. "It wasn't just a game to us—it was our way of dreaming big," Megan recalls. Those scrappy matches against older siblings and neighborhood kids forged the creativity and resilience that would later define her style of play.

As a teen, Megan idolized bold players like Diego Maradona. "He made the game an art form," she said. "I wanted to play like that—fearless, expressive, unapologetically myself." That spirit carried her to the University of Portland, where she overcame early injuries to shine as a standout talent, and eventually to the U.S. Women's National Team, where her leadership would take center stage.

One of her defining moments came during the 2019 FIFA

Women's World Cup. In the quarterfinal against host nation France, with 50,000 roaring fans watching, Megan delivered a stunning free kick in the fifth minute, silencing the crowd. "You live for those moments," she said. But it was the final against the Netherlands that became the ultimate stage. With the score tied and tension building, Megan approached the penalty spot, unshakable and calm.

The whistle blew. She exhaled, took a stride and struck the ball low and fast, past the goalkeeper's outstretched fingers. The world held its breath for a moment, then erupted as the net rippled. Megan stood still, arms outstretched, her head tilted back in triumph, a sly grin on her face. It wasn't just a goal; it was a statement. "I belong here. We belong here."

The fire she ignited carried the U.S. team to victory. Megan walked away as the tournament's top scorer and MVP, claiming the Golden Boot and Golden Ball. But for her, it was about more than soccer. "That World Cup wasn't just about winning," she said. "It was about showing the world what we stand for—and what we refuse to accept."

Off the field, Megan became a fearless advocate for change. In 2016, she knelt in solidarity with Colin Kaepernick during the national anthem, standing up against racial injustice. "It wasn't an easy choice," she admitted. "But how could I stand when so many people don't have the same freedoms I do?" The backlash only fueled her resolve.

As an openly gay athlete, Megan became a beacon for the LGBTQ+ community, encouraging others to embrace their true selves. She spearheaded the fight for equal pay in women's sports, playing a pivotal role in the U.S. Women's National Team's landmark 2022 agreement for pay equity. "We weren't just fighting for ourselves," she said. "We were fighting for future generations."

Her influence has reached far beyond soccer. From fiery speeches at the White House to her memoir, *One Life*, Megan

challenges people to act. "Real change starts with everyday choices," she writes. "It's in how we treat others, what we stand for and
what we refuse to ignore."

Megan Rapinoe's legacy isn't just about goals or trophies—it's
about using her voice for progress. She is a champion, a trailblazer
and a reminder that one person's courage can spark lasting change.
"We all have a role to play," she says. "The question is, how bold
are you willing to be?"

Anthony Joshua's journey from a restless youth in Watford,
England, to a world champion boxer exemplifies backbone and
belief. Born to Nigerian parents, he veered close to trouble as a
teenager. At 18, discovering boxing transformed him. "Boxing
didn't just change me—it saved me," Joshua recalls, emphasizing
the sport's role in forging his path to redemption and success

Starting late in boxing, Anthony Joshua turned his challenges
into his driving force. His exceptional talent and relentless determination saw him ascend the amateur ranks swiftly. At the 2012
London Olympics, buoyed by a supportive home crowd, Joshua's
performance was emblematic of his journey. In a tension-filled
final, he overcame an early setback with remarkable resilience,
clinching the gold medal. "This isn't just for me," he choked out
afterward, his voice breaking, eyes tearing. "This is for my family,
my country and everyone who believed in me." That gold didn't
just mark him as an Olympic champion—it introduced him as
boxing's next great star.

Joshua transitioned to the professional ranks with explosive
power and composure. His breakout came in 2016 when he faced
Charles Martin for the IBF heavyweight title. In just the second
round, Joshua saw his opening and landed a thunderous right
hand that sent Martin to the canvas. Moments later, another
devastating blow sealed the victory. "That was just the beginning,"
he told reporters. "I'm here to make history."

Joshua cemented his place in boxing lore the following year

with a historic clash against the legendary Wladimir Klitschko at Wembley Stadium. In front of 90,000 fans, Joshua faced his toughest test. A brutal sixth-round right hand from Klitschko knocked him down, leaving the crowd stunned. "I remember thinking, 'Get up. This isn't how it ends,'" Joshua later recalled. Rising to his feet, he weathered the storm before mounting a spectacular comeback. In the 11th round, a flurry of punches overwhelmed Klitschko, earning Joshua a stunning TKO victory and unifying the heavyweight titles.

But boxing is as much about setbacks as triumphs. In 2019, Joshua suffered a shocking defeat to Andy Ruiz Jr., a loss that stunned the sport and raised questions about his future. Instead of crumbling, Joshua embraced the lesson. "Losing teaches you more than winning ever will," he said. Six months later, in their rematch, Joshua silenced the doubters. He reclaimed his titles using strategy, discipline and composure, proving that his mental toughness matched his physical power. "The mental is more important than the physical," he reflected. "That voice in your head telling you to stop? That's the real opponent."

Outside the ring, Joshua's impact is equally profound. Growing up in Watford, he had witnessed the struggles faced by young people in difficult circumstances. Determined to give back, he became a vocal advocate against knife crime in London. Partnering with Steel Warriors, he helped turn confiscated knives into outdoor gyms, providing safe spaces for youth to train and channel their energy positively. Joshua often visits these gyms, speaking to kids who remind him of his younger self. "If I wasn't boxing, I might've been one of those kids," he says. "I want them to know there's always another way."

Joshua's commitment extends to Nigeria, where he proudly embraces his roots by supporting youth initiatives and community programs. Humble, respectful and determined, Joshua defies the stereotypes of boxing. "At the end of the day," he says, "it's about lifting people up—not just yourself."

Megan Rapinoe and Anthony Joshua have significantly influenced the culture of their sports, showcasing how leadership can challenge societal norms. Megan's vocal support for equality has initiated crucial conversations on inclusivity, challenging stereotypes and inspiring other athletes to promote diversity. Similarly, Anthony's advocacy for education, opportunity and personal empowerment has encouraged young people to transcend their circumstances, pushing for a broader perspective on achievement. Through their actions, Megan and Anthony exemplify the power of using one's platform to drive social change, showing how championing equity can help create opportunities for everyone.

AGAINST THE GRAIN: HOW ARTHUR ASHE AND YUNA KIM CHALLENGED NORMS

Arthur Ashe was more than a tennis star—he was a revolutionary, a man who broke barriers and redefined what it meant to be an athlete with a cause. Born in Richmond, Virginia, in 1943, Ashe grew up in the segregated South, where black players had few opportunities to access proper courts or coaching. His sanctuary was a small public park with a makeshift court, where he practiced tirelessly, often against wooden boards. "That court was my sanctuary," he once said. "It's where I learned discipline, focus and perseverance."

At just 10 years old, Ashe's talent caught the attention of Dr. Robert Walter Johnson, the renowned coach who had mentored Althea Gibson. Under Johnson's guidance, Ashe developed a cerebral, graceful playing style that relied more on strategy than raw power. "Dr. Johnson taught me that strategy wins matches, not just strength," he recalled. His calm demeanor—always collected and unshakable—became his trademark, masking a fierce competitive spirit underneath.

Ashe's breakthrough came in 1968, a year of immense social and political upheaval. The assassinations of Dr. Martin Luther King Jr. and Robert Kennedy, urban unrest and the growing urgency of the civil rights movement defined the moment. Against this backdrop, Ashe stepped onto the courts of the US Open, the first black man to compete at that level. Playing as an amateur, he carried immense pressure—the weight of history and the hopes of an entire community on his shoulders. Yet, Ashe played with poise and determination.

When the final point was won, the crowd erupted. Ashe had made history, becoming the first black man to win the US Open title. "I felt like I wasn't just playing for myself," he later said. "I was carrying the hopes of an entire community." The victory was more than a personal achievement; it was a symbolic moment in the fight for racial equality and a turning point for tennis.

His greatest triumph came in 1975 at Wimbledon, where he faced the brash, heavily favored Jimmy Connors. Analysts predicted a lopsided victory for Connors, but Ashe had other plans. Relying on strategy instead of brute force, he dismantled Connors' aggressive style with precision and control. "I knew I couldn't out muscle him," Ashe said. "So I had to out think him." The victory remains one of the most celebrated upsets in tennis history, cementing Ashe as a legend with three Grand Slam titles.

Yet, Ashe's greatest work unfolded off the court. A fierce advocate for civil rights, he used his platform to challenge injustice. He spoke out against apartheid in South Africa, refusing to play in the country and denouncing its racist policies. In 1992, he was arrested during a protest outside the White House, a moment that symbolized his unwavering commitment to justice. "I don't mind being remembered as a tennis player," Ashe said. "But I'd rather be remembered for fighting for human rights."

In the 1980s, Ashe faced his toughest opponent yet: a diagnosis of HIV, contracted from a blood transfusion during heart surgery. Refusing to hide, he announced his condition publicly in 1992, using his voice to fight the stigma surrounding AIDS. "I don't want pity," he declared. "I want understanding." Ashe's bravery during this period inspired millions and turned his private battle into a public cause for awareness and education.

Arthur Ashe's life was a masterclass in resilience, intellect and activism. His quiet courage shattered racial barriers and proved that greatness extends beyond sports. "True heroism," he once said, "is not the urge to surpass all others but the urge to serve others."

Yuna Kim, affectionately known as "Queen Yuna," didn't just dominate figure skating—she transformed it. Born in a small town in South Korea, her rise to the pinnacle of a sport traditionally ruled by Russia, Japan and the United States seemed improbable. Yet, with her natural talent, tireless work ethic and quiet determination, Yuna rewrote the story of what a champion could be.

Yuna Kim's journey to global stardom is a testament to her resilience and talent. Training in overcrowded rinks on bumpy ice with secondhand skates, she found freedom in figure skating and her potential was quickly recognized by her coach. As a teenager, Yuna captivated the world with her technical skill and emotional performances, turning her routines into narratives on ice. Her signature triple lutz-triple toe loop combination showcased her exceptional precision, establishing her as a figure skating icon.

Her crowning moment came at the 2010 Winter Olympics in Vancouver. In her short program set to Gershwin's *Concerto in F*, Yuna moved with unmatched grace, each step a seamless blend of power and elegance. She launched into her triple-triple combination, nailing it with an effortlessness that made the impossible look routine.

Her free skate to *Adiós Nonino* was transcendent—a performance filled with vulnerability and strength. Her jumps soared, her spins flowed like poetry and her storytelling drew the audience into a world of beauty and heartbreak. When she struck her final pose, the arena erupted in a mix of awe and emotion.

The scoreboard lit up: 228.56—a new world record. Yuna had won Olympic gold, delivering what is still considered one of the greatest performances in figure skating history. "I didn't skate just for gold," she later said. "I skated for my country, for everyone who believed in me." Overnight, Yuna became a champion and a cultural icon, igniting a figure skating renaissance in South Korea. Thousands of young girls laced up their skates, inspired by the queen who had shown them what was possible.

But her journey wasn't without its struggles. Injuries tested her body and the immense pressure of carrying a nation's hopes weighed heavily. "There were times I wanted to quit," she admitted. "But I remembered why I started." Her resilience shone once again at the 2014 Sochi Olympics, where she earned silver in a performance that reinforced her grace and grit. Though not gold, her composure under pressure only solidified her enduring legacy.

Off the ice, Yuna Kim's influence has extended far beyond sports. As a UNICEF Goodwill Ambassador, she has used her platform to advocate for children's rights, education and global disaster relief. After the 2010 Haiti earthquake, Yuna donated her entire prize money to aid recovery efforts, saying, "These children have lost everything. It's our duty to help them rebuild their lives." Her generosity has consistently changed lives, from supporting flood victims in Korea to contributing to typhoon recovery in the Philippines.

Yuna has also been a vocal advocate for education, particularly for young girls. "The ice gave me a platform," she often says. "Now it's my turn to give back." Her work has opened doors for underprivileged children, ensuring they, too, have a chance to thrive.

Arthur Ashe and Yuna Kim leveraged their athletic prowess to champion broader causes. Ashe challenged systemic racism, was a vocal opponent of apartheid and worked tirelessly to combat the stigma surrounding HIV/AIDS. At the same time, Kim served as a UNICEF Goodwill Ambassador to advocate for children's welfare and has ardently supported disaster recovery efforts. Their endeavors transcended their sports, tackling critical global issues, challenging entrenched social norms and promoting a culture of inclusivity. Ashe's dignified stance against racial discrimination and Kim's breakthrough in a traditionally less accessible sport for athletes from her region demonstrate the profound impact of using one's success for societal progress.

INTERCONNECTING THE STORIES OF DIVERSITY AND BREAKING BARRIERS OF OUR SIX ATHLETES

The narratives of Muhammad Ali, Roberto Clemente, Megan Rapinoe, Anthony Joshua, Arthur Ashe and Yuna Kim weave together personal drive, courage and the desire to effect societal change, highlighting the influential role of sports in advocating for social justice and inclusion. Their stories transcend their achievements, illustrating the impact of using one's platform to challenge cultural norms and promote diversity and fairness. Ali and Rapinoe powerfully demonstrate the significance of speaking out for social justice, using their fame to combat racial inequality and fight for LGBTQ+ rights. Their commitments to advocacy bring to light the amplified potential of sports heroes as agents of change. Clemente and Joshua, through their dedication to community uplift and outreach, showcase how athletic success can be a force for inclusion, opening doors for marginalized communities. Their efforts underscore the power of leveraging great personal achievement to foster a more inclusive society. Ashe and Kim embody the spirit of blending accomplishment with advocacy, breaking cultural barriers and using their prominence to champion causes beyond their sports. Their legacies inspire a commitment to equality and the courage to challenge the status quo. These athletes' amazing stories teach us the value of breaking barriers not just for personal triumph but for inspiring and creating a more inclusive world.

––––––

REFLECTION: HOW CAN YOU BE A CHAMPION FOR CHANGE?

The stories in this chapter remind us that the fight for inclusion, equality and diversity requires courage, resilience and action. Each athlete showed us that while breaking barriers is never easy, it is gratifying—not just for oneself but for the generations that follow. Use these questions to reflect on your role in fostering diversity, equality and opportunity:

• *Your Platform:* Muhammad Ali and Megan Rapinoe used their voices to advocate for justice. What platforms or opportunities do you have in your life—whether in school, your community or social media—where you can speak up for fairness and inclusion? Are you using them to their fullest potential?

• *Empathy and Understanding:* Arthur Ashe and Yuna Kim bridged cultural divides through their actions and words. Have you ever experienced a moment when gaining a deeper understanding of someone different from yourself challenged or shifted your perspective? How can a deeper empathy for others guide you in breaking down barriers?

• *Leading Locally:* Roberto Clemente and Anthony Joshua made a difference in their communities by using their influence to uplift others. What small actions can you take to create a more inclusive environment in your school, team or neighborhood?

• *Overcoming Personal Barriers:* Diversity is about embracing the unique qualities that make someone who they are. Have you ever felt excluded or held back because of who you are? How did you respond and what did you learn about yourself? How can that experience help you support others?

ACTION PLAN: TAKING STEPS TOWARD INCLUSION

• *Expand Your Circle:* Challenge yourself to connect with someone different from you—someone from another background, culture or group. Start with a simple conversation to learn more about their experiences. Broadening your perspective is the first step toward promoting inclusion.

• *Speak Up:* If you see someone being mistreated, find a way to speak up or offer support. It could be as simple as standing up for a classmate, reporting bullying or starting a discussion about fairness. Take inspiration from Megan Rapinoe's courage in addressing uncomfortable truths.

• *Celebrate Diversity:* Organize or participate in activities that celebrate diversity—such as cultural appreciation events, book clubs featuring diverse authors or team-building exercises focused on inclusion. Highlighting differences helps build unity.

• *Give Back:* Volunteer for a cause that aligns with your values. Whether it's mentoring younger kids, supporting an LGBTQ+ advocacy group or participating in community cleanup efforts, your actions can inspire others, just like Clemente and Joshua's dedication to their communities.

• *Create Inclusive Spaces:* Reflect on the groups or activities you're part of. Are they welcoming to everyone? If not, think of ways to make them more inclusive. For example, if you're on a sports team or in a club, suggest team-building activities that encourage camaraderie and understanding among all members.

• *Educate Yourself:* Read about or watch documentaries on the challenges faced by marginalized groups. For instance, learning about Arthur Ashe's activism against apartheid or Muhammad Ali's stance on civil rights can deepen your understanding of social justice issues.

• *Practice Daily Acts of Inclusion:* Inclusion starts with small, intentional actions—like inviting someone who feels left out to join a conversation or group, actively listening to someone's story or simply showing kindness to someone who might feel isolated.

• *Share Your Story:* Just as these athletes used their stories to inspire change, consider sharing your own experiences of overcoming barriers or witnessing inequality. Your voice, no matter how small it may seem, can have a powerful ripple effect.

A final thought: Be the change you want to see. The athletes in this chapter remind us that breaking barriers is a continuous journey. Whether it's standing up for a cause, advocating for someone else or creating inclusive spaces, each action matters. You don't need to be famous to make a difference; you just need courage, compassion and the belief that your efforts, no matter how small, can create meaningful change. Reflect, act and let your life be a testament to the power of diversity and inclusion.

6 REDEMPTION AND SECOND CHANCES

FROM FALLEN STAR TO ROLE MODEL: THE REDEMPTION OF ALLEN IVERSON AND HOPE SOLO

ALLEN IVERSON WASN'T JUST a basketball player—he was a storm in sneakers, a cultural force crammed into a six-foot frame. To his fans, he was "The Answer," a name that fit him as perfectly as his crazy fast crossover. But his story wasn't built on pristine hardwood—it was forged in the grit of Hampton, Virginia, where the odds were stacked high.

Raised by his mother, Ann, in a cramped apartment where running water was a luxury, survival shaped Iverson's every move. "Allen always fought," Ann said. "He had no choice." Sports became his outlet. At Bethel High School, Iverson first made his name—not in basketball, but as a star quarterback, leading his team to a state championship. "AI was like a magician out there," his coach recalled. "He did things you couldn't explain."

But at 17, everything came crashing down. A bowling alley

brawl landed Iverson in the center of a controversial case that many believed was fueled by racial bias. Despite conflicting accounts, Iverson was convicted and sentenced to five years in prison. The punishment sparked outrage, and for Iverson, the experience was devastating. "I thought my life was over," he later admitted. "Everything I worked for was gone."

After four months, public pressure led to clemency from the Virginia governor. The ordeal left scars but also revealed his resilience. "It broke me," Iverson said years later. "But it also made me."

Enter John Thompson Jr., the legendary Georgetown coach who saw something others overlooked. At their first meeting, Thompson's words were direct: "I'm going to save your life." And he did. Under Thompson's mentorship, Iverson thrived, becoming a two-time Defensive Player of the Year. He redefined the expectations of a six-foot guard, blending unrelenting energy, speed and toughness into a style no one could match.

In the 1996 draft, the Philadelphia 76ers chose Iverson first and the NBA would never be the same. His signature lightning-quick crossover dribble left defenders stumbling, most famously Michael Jordan during Iverson's rookie year. "I wasn't scared," Iverson later said. "I was just being me."

By 2001, Iverson carried the Sixers to the NBA Finals, putting his team on his back. In Game 1 against the powerhouse Los Angeles Lakers, Iverson dropped 48 points, including the iconic jumper over Tyronn Lue, punctuated by the step-over—a moment of swagger that became legend. "That was Allen," said teammate Eric Snow. "All heart, no fear."

Off the court, Iverson shattered the NBA's image. With his cornrows, tattoos and baggy clothes, he brought hip-hop and street culture into the spotlight. To some, he was rebellious. To his fans, he was real. The infamous "practice" press conference, where

Iverson mockingly repeated the word "practice" twenty two times, symbolized his frustration and defiance. Critics called him difficult, but millions saw him as someone who refused to be anyone but himself.

"People loved Allen because he was them," said former Sixers GM Billy King. "He wasn't perfect but he was honest." Even NBA superstar Kevin Durant later said, "AI made it okay to be yourself."

Iverson's career was as turbulent as it was brilliant. Clashes with coaches, financial struggles and personal battles made him a flawed but fiercely human figure. His brilliance on the court and raw authenticity off it created a connection with fans that transcended basketball.

Through triumphs and trials, Iverson's legacy is undeniable. "I gave everything I had," he once said. "And I did it my way." His story reminds us that greatness doesn't come from perfection—it comes from the fight.

Beyond her role as a goalkeeper, Hope Solo was a dynamic force in soccer, known for her commanding presence and unwavering determination. With the U.S. Women's National Team, she not only earned two Olympic golds and a World Cup title but also revolutionized the role of a goalkeeper with her exceptional athleticism and tenacity.

Growing up in Richland, Washington, Hope Solo faced a challenging childhood. Her father grappled with homelessness and legal troubles, but he instilled in her resilience and taught her to confront challenges directly. Soccer became her refuge and her calling. Initially shining as a forward in high school, a shift to goalkeeper at the University of Washington revealed her true potential, paving the way for her illustrious career.

In college, she quickly established herself as one of the best, setting records and showcasing her rock-solid confidence. Her talent wasn't the only thing that set her apart—her fiery determination was also important. Her college coach recalled, "Hope wasn't just trying to stop goals; she wanted to dominate every game. Her hunger was unmatched."

By the mid-2000s, Hope Solo became a pillar for the U.S. Women's National Team as its starting goalkeeper, shining brightest on the world stage. Her standout performance in the 2008 Olympics' final against Brazil clinched gold for the team. "I live for these moments," she stated, victorious and resolute. In 2012, Hope's excellence was on display again as she anchored the team's defense to secure a gold medal against Japan. Teammate Abby Wambach observed, "She thrives under pressure. The bigger the stakes, the better Hope plays."

In the 2015 FIFA Women's World Cup, Hope shone brilliantly, conceding just three goals throughout the tournament. Her exceptional saves, particularly in the critical knockout stages, captivated fans and frustrated adversaries alike. Her prowess was on full display in the final against Japan, where she was a key factor in the U.S. team's dominant performance, securing their first World Cup win in 16 years. After the final whistle, an emotional Solo reflected on the victory, stating, "This is why I play. For moments like this."

Yet Solo's life off the field was as fiery and unpredictable as her performance on it. Known for her unapologetic honesty and fierce independence, Solo often found herself at odds with those around her. She clashed openly with coaches, teammates and the media, her blunt words sparking admiration and controversy. "I've never been afraid to speak my mind," she declared. It's who I am."

The turbulence peaked in 2014 when Solo was arrested on domestic violence charges after a family altercation, an event that sparked public debate. Critics saw it as proof of her volatility, while supporters argued it underscored the disproportionate scrutiny female athletes face. "They see the headlines," Solo remarked, "but they don't see the whole story."

Her conflict with the U.S. Soccer Federation over gender pay equality further fueled the controversy. As a leading voice against pay disparities, Solo became a contentious figure. Some admired her bravery, while others criticized her direct approach. Nonetheless, she stood firm, stating, "I'm not here to be perfect; I'm here to fight for what's right."

Despite the controversies, Solo's impact on the sport is undeniable. She elevated the goalkeeper role, inspiring countless young players to see the position as one of power and influence. "Hope changed the game," a former teammate said. "She made us believe that anything was possible."

Allen Iverson and Hope Solo were more than modern athletes —they were mavericks who turned trials into transformation. Iverson's unapologetic authenticity and journey from controversy to Hall of Fame status proved the power of individuality and an unyielding spirit, inspiring change on and off the court. Similarly, Solo's fearless advocacy for gender equality and her unstoppable will turned personal struggles into progress and reshaped women's sports. Both faced adversity with fiery independence, teaching young readers that embracing imperfections and tackling challenges head-on leads to growth. Their legacies remind us that redemption is often about more than personal triumph—it's about making a lasting impact on the world.

TURNING THE PAGE: THE COMEBACK STORIES OF ALEX RODRIGUEZ AND MARION JONES

Raised in Washington Heights, New York, and later in Miami, Alex Rodriguez found his place in baseball from a young age, a passion inherited from his Dominican pro-player father. After his father left when Alex was ten, baseball became his refuge. His exceptional talent shone brightly in high school, where his remarkable swing and speed won him the Gatorade National Baseball Player of the Year and led his team to a state championship. At just 17, Rodriguez was the first overall pick in the 1993 MLB Draft by the Seattle Mariners, embarking on a journey that would dramatically impact baseball's history.

Alex's ascent was meteoric. By 1996, his second full season in the majors, the 20-year-old shortstop was rewriting the record books. He hit .358 with 36 home runs and 123 RBIs, becoming the youngest player to lead the American League in batting average. "It felt like I was playing in a dream," Alex said of that season. His blend of power, speed and defensive wizardry revolutionized the shortstop position, proving it could be both a defensive stronghold and an offensive powerhouse.

Alex's talent commanded unprecedented value. The Texas Rangers signed him in 2001 to a record-breaking $252 million contract, the largest in sports history at that time. The move fixed him in place as the face of baseball. Over the next three seasons, he earned three consecutive home run titles, dazzling fans with his ability to make the absolutely extraordinary look almost routine.

The allure of New York presented unprecedented opportunities and challenges for Rodriguez after joining the Yankees in 2004. Amidst intense scrutiny and pressure, he secured two MVP awards in 2005 and 2007, establishing his status among baseball's luminaries. However, his pivotal role in the Yankees' 2009 World Series victory, overcoming past postseason disappointments and silencing critics, truly defined his tenure in New York. "This is why I came to New York," he declared, lifting the championship trophy triumphantly.

However, Alex's career faced significant turmoil. In 2009, he confessed to using performance-enhancing drugs (PEDs) during his time with the Texas Rangers, a revelation that stunned fans and critics, undermining his achievements. "I was young and made a terrible decision," Alex expressed regretfully. This confession was just the beginning. In 2013, the Biogenesis scandal further entangled him in controversy, making him a central figure in a doping investigation that shook Major League Baseball. Accused of lying about his PED use and obstructing the league's investigation, he faced a historic 162-game suspension, sidelining him for the entire 2014 season and threatening his legacy.

The weight of it all—public scrutiny, personal shame and the betrayal felt by fans—was immense. "I made mistakes," he admitted with a rare vulnerability. "But I'm determined to write a better ending to my story."

And he did. In 2015, Alex Rodriguez staged an impressive comeback, defying skeptics with a year after suspension. At 39, he smashed 33 homers and notched 86 RBIs, showcasing his enduring capabilities. "I was proving to myself I could still contribute," he said.

Beyond the diamond, Rodriguez made great efforts to transform himself. Diving into business, he cultivated a successful real estate empire and emerged as a sought-after TV analyst, often praised for his insights into the game. Crucially, he became a mentor, sharing lessons from his storied career. "Baseball gave me everything," he mused, "and now, it's my turn to give back."

Marion Jones was the epitome of excellence at the 2000 Sydney Olympics, dominating the track with her speed and capturing three gold and two bronze medals. Her victories broke barriers and set new standards for women and African Americans in sports. "This is what I've dreamed of," she remarked, her superb Olympic achievements a marker of her athletic brilliance.

Behind her global success was a complex story. Growing up in Los Angeles, Marion quickly outpaced boys on the playground, showcasing her early talent. Raised by a hardworking single mother from Belize, Marion learned the value of ambition and perseverance. "Her sacrifices taught me to dream big," she reflected.

As a high school sensation, Marion's rise was meteoric. She outpaced track competitors with unmatched speed and dominated the basketball court, captivating audiences with her skill. However, her rapid success brought mounting expectations, making each victory a heavier burden to carry.

At the University of North Carolina, Marion's brilliance reached new heights. Crowds filled arenas and tracks to witness her in action while the media buzzed about her unstoppable talent and magnetic presence. She became more than an athlete—she was a symbol, a beacon of excellence. But that spotlight burned very, very hot. "Everyone expected me to be perfect," she later confessed, her voice tinged with the weariness of hindsight. "But perfection isn't real—it's a trap, and I walked right into it."

The trap snapped shut after the Olympics. The spotlight grew harsher, the scrutiny sharper. To many, Marion appeared invincible, but behind the scenes, she wrestled with the unrelenting demands of staying on top. Her victories brought fame and fortune, but they also brought whispers—whispers of doping, whispers she denied fiercely for years. "I didn't want to let anyone down," she later said. "But the pressure was crushing."

In 2007, the weight of the truth came crashing down. Marion tearfully admitted to using performance-enhancing drugs (PEDs) after federal prosecutors confronted her with evidence, including testimony from witnesses and documents linking her to the use of the illegal drug. This represented a clear betrayal of trust that rocked the sports world. Her five Olympic medals were stripped and her achievements were erased from history. "I have let you down," she confessed in a public apology, her voice trembling. "I have let my family down. I have let myself down."

The fallout didn't end there. Marion faced legal consequences for lying to federal investigators during the BALCO doping scandal. The courtroom was packed as the once-celebrated star stood before a judge and received a six-month prison sentence. "Hearing that gavel hit—it was like my world shattered," she later said. Her time behind bars became a stark reckoning, forcing her to confront not just the choices she'd made but the person she wanted to become.

When Marion emerged, the world had moved on, but she hadn't given up on herself. She shares her story through public speaking, mentoring and her memoir, "On the Right Track." Marion speaks at schools, sports camps and conferences, using her experiences to caution young athletes about the dangers of short-cuts and the importance of integrity. "I want them to know the cost of shortcuts," she said. In her talks, she addresses the pressures of fame, her mistakes and her path to redemption, often saying, "Your talent can take you to the top, but only your character will keep you there."

Despite facing intense public scrutiny and personal challenges, Alex Rodriguez and Marion Jones transfigured their difficulties into pathways for personal growth. Alex refined his focus on rebuilding trust and accountability, making a remarkable come-back in baseball and later thriving as a sports analyst and entrepreneur. His work in broadcasting, philanthropy and mentorship played a key role in restoring his public image. In parallel, Marion confronted her previous errors head-on, lever-aging motivational speaking and community service to underscore the value of integrity and the possibility of a fresh start. Demon-strating genuine regret and bravery, both athletes proved that while mistakes carry weight, they don't dictate our entire story.

RISING AGAIN: BEN COUSINS AND DIEGO MARADONA'S SEARCH FOR REDEMPTION

Ben Cousins stood out as a footballer and an extraordinary talent. His agility and intuitive game sense made him exceptional, captivating fans who filled stadiums to witness his dynamic play. As the West Coast Eagles' captain, he led his team to a 2006 premiership, cementing his status among the legends of Australian Rules Football. Former teammates praised him, highlighting his skill, determination and effortless leadership.

Growing up in a football dynasty, Ben Cousins was earmarked for greatness early on. His father, Bryan, a revered figure at the Perth Football Club, introduced Ben to the game, igniting a passion that would define his future. "I just wanted to be like Dad," Ben reminisced, admiring his father's prowess on the field. Ben's journey, however, was not merely a continuation of his father's legacy but a quest to carve out his own. His natural aptitude for the game—marked by exceptional speed, endurance and instinct—soon caught the attention of scouts. Deemed a once-in-a-generation talent, he was drafted by the West Coast Eagles at the age of 17. Ben's debut was spectacular, captivating fans with his intense play and off-field charisma, rapidly becoming a luminary in the AFL.

In 2005, Ben reached the pinnacle of his sport's success, claiming the Brownlow Medal, the AFL's most prestigious honor. "It's every kid's dream," he said during his acceptance speech, cradling the medal as cheers erupted around him. The award wasn't just a symbol of his dominance—it was confirmation that he had become the player everyone had envisioned and more. Ben Cousins wasn't just a footballer; he was the embodiment of excellence, a national icon whose brilliance on the field inspired countless fans.

As accolades accumulated, so did the pressures of fame, intensifying Ben's secret battle with drug addiction. "I thought I could control it," he confessed, reflecting on his misguided belief that fame's trappings wouldn't overtake him. However, by 2006, his off-field issues began to overshadow his on-field achievements, leading to erratic behavior and unexplained absences that caught the media's attention.

By 2007, the full weight of Ben Cousins' personal battles came crashing down in a very public way. The West Coast Eagles, the team with which he had soared to the heights of his career, made the difficult decision to release him. Cousins himself described this moment as "rock bottom," a low point from which the only way forward was either a steep climb back or further descent into his struggles. The aftermath was rapid and unforgiving, with arrests and legal challenges quickly piling up. These incidents were splashed across headlines, casting a long shadow over the legacy of a once-revered athlete.

In 2009, Cousins made a brief comeback with the Richmond Tigers, showing glimpses of the player he once was. Fans cheered his resilience, hoping for redemption. But the weight of his past was impossible to escape. "I'd get on the field and feel like myself again," he reflected. "But off the field, it was a different story." His return was short-lived, and his career ended not with a triumphant farewell but with the lingering shadow of what could have been.

Despite his challenges, Ben Cousins' story transcends caution, offering insights into the pressures athletes endure and their vulnerabilities. His journey illuminated the critical need for enhanced mental health and addiction support within sports. Now, his relentless pursuit of recovery and personal growth stands as a beacon of hope, encapsulated in his own words: "I'm still fighting."

On the dusty streets of Villa Fiorito, a slum in Buenos Aires, a young Diego Maradona first fell in love with soccer. With a worn-out ball between his feet, he mesmerized neighbors as he weaved through makeshift goals and danced past opponents, his left foot an instrument of magic. "That boy will be a star," one coach predicted after seeing him play at just eight years old.

When he joined the Argentinos Juniors at age 15, Maradona was already hailed as a prodigy. His rise was meteoric: at 16, he debuted for the Argentine national team, his dazzling footwork and vision drawing comparisons to the greatest players of all time. "I felt like I was carrying my entire neighborhood with me," he once said, a sentiment that would define his career.

Maradona's crowning moment came during the 1986 FIFA World Cup in Mexico, a tournament that fixed his place in history. It was in the quarterfinals against England that Diego delivered two moments that would define the duality of his character. The first, the infamous "Hand of God," showcased his audacity. As he leapt for the ball, he punched it into the net with his hand, fooling the officials. "A little with the head of Maradona and a little with the hand of God," he cheekily quipped afterward.

Minutes later, Maradona executed the "Goal of the Century," a masterpiece in soccer history. From his own half, he dashed solo, dancing past the English defense with almost supernatural agility. As he glided past the goalkeeper to score, the crowd was spell-bound, witnessing not just a goal but an art form. "It felt like the world stopped," teammate Jorge Valdano said, encapsulating Maradona's magic in that unforgettable play.

Diego's time at Napoli, in Italy, solidified his legendary status. Arriving in 1984, he transformed the struggling club into champions, leading them to two Serie A titles and a UEFA Cup victory. Diego was more than a footballer for the people of Naples—he was a savior. Murals of his face adorned walls and children in the poorest neighborhoods wore his number 10 jersey as a badge of hope. "He gave us dignity," a Neapolitan fan once said.

But for all his brilliance, Maradona's life was a kaleidoscope of triumphs and trials. His battles with addiction shadowed his career, leading to periods of unpredictable behavior and suspensions. "I made mistakes," he later confessed, "but football was my salvation." Despite his struggles, Maradona's impact on soccer was profound. With his undeniable charisma and passion, he transcended the sport, embodying both the fragility and the resilience of the human spirit. His journey, marked by extraordinary peaks and deep valleys, showcased a life lived with intensity, making him an enduring icon to fans worldwide.

In his later years, Maradona sought redemption, embracing his flaws and using his platform to connect with those who idolized him. Whether coaching, speaking or simply showing up in the neighborhoods that worshiped his legacy, he reminded the world that the essence of redemption is not about erasing mistakes but, perhaps, simply learning from them and maintaining the will to do better. His life is a testament to the enduring power of passion and the possibility of renewal, showing that greatness and redemption can coexist even amidst chaos.

Ben Cousins and Diego Maradona each endured deep personal low points and faced pivotal moments when change was imperative for survival. Cousins embarked on a path of recovery, leveraging his journey to advocate for mental health and addiction support, becoming a symbol of hope. Maradona, battling health issues from substance abuse, worked to reshape his public image and break the stigma around addiction. Their advocacy not only contributed to their legacies but also offered lessons in resolve and the possibility of redemption despite severe setbacks. Both athletes used their platforms to foster change and inspire hope, demonstrating that, with determination, overcoming even the most daunting challenges is within reach.

INTERCONNECTING THE REDEMPTION STORIES OF THE SIX ATHLETES

In the high-stakes world of professional sports, the path to redemption is often as public as it is personal, all on display for the critical eyes of fans and media alike. Athletes like Allen Iverson, Hope Solo, Alex Rodriguez, Marion Jones, Ben Cousins and Diego Maradona have each navigated this journey, confronting challenges ranging from legal issues and substance abuse to doping scandals. Despite these varied obstacles, their stories converge on themes of accountability, humility and the drive to regain trust and credibility. Their experiences underscore the severe repercussions of mistakes, yet also the profound courage required to take them on openly and authentically. Each athlete reaches a pivotal moment when he or she chooses to confront reality, take responsibility and push for positive change. This critical decision set the stage for their personal and public redemption, highlighting the vital importance of transparency and accountability. Their stories also reveal that for public figures, redemption goes beyond personal transformation and also includes the extra duty to give back to the community. Whether mentoring young athletes, engaging in advocacy or sharing their stories to educate others, these sports figures transformed their trials into platforms for inspiring change and empowering others. The collective narratives of Iverson, Solo, Rodriguez, Jones, Cousins and Maradona demonstrate redemption's transformative power. Despite unyielding attention and the challenges of rebuilding their lives and reputations, their durability and commitment to self-improvement stand out. They remind us that while our mistakes may influence how we're perceived, they don't have to define our legacy. Embracing humility and learning from our errors opens the path to redemption.

—————

REFLECTION: OWNING YOUR STORY

Redemption begins with facing the truth about our actions and the consequences they bring. The athletes in this chapter teach us that the road to redemption is rarely smooth but it is always transformative. Reflect on these questions to explore how these stories connect to your own experiences:

• *Facing Mistakes:* Allen Iverson and Marion Jones made choices that led to significant consequences but found the courage to take responsibility. Think about a mistake you've made—big or small. How did you handle it? Did you own up to it or did you avoid it? What might you do differently next time?

• *Confronting Public Judgment:* Hope Solo and Alex Rodriguez faced intense public scrutiny for their actions. Have you ever felt judged for a decision you made? How did you deal with that pressure? What did it teach you about resilience?

• *The Power of a Fresh Start:* Ben Cousins and Diego Maradona showed that redemption is about more than words—it's about consistent actions to rebuild trust. Are there relationships or situations in your life that need rebuilding? What steps can you take to show others you're committed to change?

• *Using Lessons to Inspire:* Many of these athletes turned their struggles into opportunities to mentor and educate others. How can the challenges you've faced be a source of inspiration for others? How might sharing your story help someone else on their journey?

Take a moment to write down your reflections on redemption. These thoughts will guide you in considering how to approach your own opportunities for growth and redemption.

ACTION PLAN: WALKING THE PATH OF REDEMPTION

• *Acknowledge and Accept:* Reflect on a mistake or regret that weighs on you. Write it down in your private journal, being honest about what happened and how it made you feel. Accepting responsibility is the first step toward redemption, just as it was for these athletes.

• *Apologize and Make Amends:* Consider how you can make amends if your actions hurt someone. You can write a letter, have a conversation or take a tangible action to repair the relationship. Genuine apologies can be a powerful step in rebuilding trust.

• *Set a Redemption Goal:* Choose one area of your life where you'd like to improve—rebuilding a relationship, changing a habit or proving your commitment to a goal. Break it into small, actionable steps and track your progress.

• *Focus on Consistent Actions:* Redemption isn't about a single moment of change—it's about showing up every day with a renewed commitment to improvement. Make a list of daily or weekly actions that reflect your dedication, whether it's being more reliable, practicing kindness or staying disciplined.

• *Mentor or Give Back:* Just as Alex Rodriguez has mentored young athletes and Marion Jones has educated others about her journey, consider how you can use your experiences to help someone else. Volunteer, coach or simply share your story with someone who might benefit from hearing it.

• *Forgive Yourself:* Redemption also requires self-compassion. Remember that everyone makes mistakes and what matters most is how you grow from them. Write a note of forgiveness to yourself, acknowledging the past and committing to a better future.

• *Build a Support System:* Surround yourself with people who believe in your potential for change and who hold you accountable. Share your goals with them and ask for their encouragement as you work toward redemption.

• *Celebrate Progress:* Redemption is a long journey, but every small step matters. Celebrate your progress—whether it's mending a friendship, overcoming a bad habit or simply feeling more at peace with yourself. These victories remind you that change is possible.

A final thought: Redemption Is a journey, not a destination. The athletes in this chapter remind us that their paths toward renewal are about growth, not perfection. It's about showing courage in the face of errors, taking responsibility, committing to positive change and using your experiences to make a difference. No matter what you've been through, you have the power to redefine your story and leave a legacy of resilience and hope. Take a step today—however small—toward the person you want to become. Remember, it's not the mistakes that define us but how we rise after them.

7 THE POSITIVE INFLUENCE OF A MENTOR OR COACH

THE GUIDING LIGHT: HOW PHIL JACKSON AND PAT SUMMITT INSPIRED GREATNESS

PHIL JACKSON LED superstars like Michael Jordan, Scottie Pippen, Shaquille O'Neal and Kobe Bryant. He tackled the daunting task of aligning their ambitions and egos. Embracing an unconventional Zen Buddhism approach, he emphasized mindfulness, meditation and present living. This unique strategy not only clinched victories but also cultivated team unity and purpose.

Jackson's path to legendary status began in Deer Lodge, Montana, within a strict Pentecostal family where discipline reigned supreme and basketball offered solace. "It was my way of connecting to something bigger than myself," he said, laying the groundwork for his groundbreaking coaching philosophy.

During high school, Phil Jackson's standout court presence caught the New York Knicks' eye, leading to two championship wins in the 1970s. Not the flashiest player, Jackson's keen strategic mind and leadership were his hallmarks. "I was never the most talented," he conceded, "but I learned to think the game." Transitioning to coaching, he honed his philosophy in smaller leagues, including Puerto Rico, focusing on mindfulness and team cohesion. "Teaching plays isn't enough," he noted. "You need to teach players to think and connect."

In 1989, Jackson took over the Chicago Bulls, inheriting a young Michael Jordan and a team brimming with potential but lacking direction. Jackson's approach was revolutionary. He introduced the triangle offense, a system that prioritized ball movement and teamwork over individual heroics, challenging Jordan to trust his teammates. "Phil made me see the bigger picture," Jordan later said. He made me a better player by making us a better team."

But it wasn't just X's and O's that set Jackson apart—it was his ability to connect with his players on a deeper level. He saw them as individuals, not just athletes, tailoring his approach to their personalities. He assigned books like *Siddhartha* for the introspective or *The Art of War* for the fiercely competitive, using literature to spark growth and self-awareness. "Phil gave me a book that changed how I saw myself," one player said. "It wasn't just about basketball; it was about life."

Practices under Phil Jackson often commenced in silence, with mindfulness exercises to sharpen focus and center the players. He incorporated metaphors from Zen philosophy and Native American traditions in team meetings, fostering a sense of unity and emphasizing the collective goal over individual achievement. "He wasn't just coaching basketball," remarked Scottie Pippen, "He was teaching us the essence of presence and teamwork, extending well beyond the court." This fusion of strategic gameplay with personal development solidified his status as the "Zen Master" in the realm of professional sports.

Under Jackson's guidance, the Bulls became a dynasty, winning six championships in the 1990s, carving Jordan's and Pippen's legacies in the process. And Jackson's work wasn't done. In 1999, he took his philosophy west to the Los Angeles Lakers, inheriting another volatile mix of talent and egos in Kobe Bryant and Shaquille O'Neal. Where others saw tension, Jackson saw opportunity. By fostering mutual respect and keeping the team's focus on the bigger picture, he guided the Lakers to five championships, creating yet another dynasty.

Phil Jackson's impact transcended his 11 championship victories. He reshaped the culture of professional sports by emphasizing mindfulness, unity and the power of a collective vision. His philosophy, "Success begins in the mind," was brought to life through innovative practices, including silent meditations and thought-provoking literature, which encouraged his players to see beyond the court. This approach honed their athletic prowess and fostered personal growth, teamwork and resilience, imprinting a lasting legacy on both the sport and his athletes.

Pat Summitt coached women's college basketball—and she revolutionized it. Fierce, demanding and unwavering, she built the Tennessee Lady Volunteers into a hardcourt dynasty, but her legacy extended far beyond the 1,098 victories and eight national championships. It was rooted in her unrelenting philosophy: discipline, accountability and personal growth were non-negotiable. "You don't just play for Pat," said one former player. "You grow for her."

Born in Henrietta, Tennessee, Pat grew up on a dairy farm, where she learned hard work and steadfastness by rising before dawn to help her father with chores. "My dad never accepted excuses," she once said. "He taught me that you earn respect by how hard you're willing to work." That mindset shaped her future as a coach and leader.

When Pat took over the Lady Vols in 1974 at just 22 years old, the program lacked resources, recognition and respect. But Pat's vision was clear: excellence was the only standard. "We're going to work harder than anyone else," she told her players. And they did. Practices were grueling, pushing players to their mental and physical limits. She demanded accountability at every turn. Players who missed class ran laps and excuses were never tolerated. "Discipline is not a dirty word," she would say. "It's the bridge between goals and accomplishments."

Central to her program was her "Definite Dozen"—a set of principles that went far beyond basketball. From "Take full responsibility" to "Make winning an attitude," these life lessons became the foundation of her philosophy. "It wasn't just about winning games," Tamika Catchings, one of her most celebrated players, recalled. "It was about how you lived your life."

Pat's coaching wasn't just tough—it was deeply personal. She had an extraordinary ability to push players to their limits while making them feel valued. During one particularly intense practice, she pulled Chamique Holdsclaw aside after berating her for a mistake. "You're better than this," she said, her tone softening. "And I'm not going to let you settle for less." Her face was taut but her eyes warmed. That balance of fire and compassion created a culture of trust and loyalty. Her players knew she expected their best because she believed in their potential.

The results were undeniable. Under Pat's guidance, the Lady Vols became a powerhouse, winning eight national championships and producing legends like Holdsclaw and Catchings. But her players often pointed to lessons off the court as her greatest gifts. "She taught us to show up for life, no matter what," Catchings said. "To be prepared, to be disciplined and to give everything you have."

Pat's impact extended beyond her team, transforming women's basketball as a whole. She demanded respect for the women's game, pushing for better resources, higher standards and greater visibility. Her relentless pursuit of excellence set a bench-mark for coaches across all sports.

In 2011, Pat was diagnosed with early-onset Alzheimer's, a cruel twist for someone whose sharp mind had shaped the game for decades. Yet even in the face of adversity, she remained true to her philosophy, facing the disease with courage and grace.

Pat Summitt's legacy isn't just her titles or victories—it's the generations of players, coaches, and fans she inspired. She proved that leadership rooted in integrity, discipline and compassion could transform not just a team but an entire sport.

Despite their contrasting styles, Phil Jackson and Pat Summitt shared a core mission: to unleash the potential of their players. Phil's Zen-infused methods brought calm and unity to powerhouse teams like the Chicago Bulls and LA Lakers while Pat instilled a relentless work ethic and accountability in the Tennessee Lady Volunteers. Their leadership transformed talented athletes into champions and icons, such as Michael Jordan under Phil and Tamika Catchings under Pat, each leaving an indelible mark on sports leadership and culture. Their coaching philosophies underscore the essence of resilience, teamwork and adaptability—Phil teaches the power of mindfulness in high-stakes moments and Pat champions the virtues of discipline and putting the team first. Together, they exemplify the profound impact of exceptional mentorship and character development in achieving success.

NURTURING TALENT: THE TRANSFORMATIVE GUIDANCE OF CARLO ANCELOTTI AND ANSON DORRANCE

Carlo Ancelotti's journey through soccer began humbly in the quiet town of Reggiolo, Italy, where fields stretched wide and the game was more passion than profession. As a boy, Carlo would tag along with his father, a cheese maker, helping turn wheels of Parmigiano-Reggiano by day and chasing a ball through the village streets by night. "That's where I learned discipline," he later said. "And that's where I fell in love with football."

Carlo's playing career as a midfielder showcased his talent and tactical understanding, honed during his time with clubs like AS Roma and AC Milan. Under the legendary Arrigo Sacchi at Milan, Carlo absorbed a vision of the game that balanced precision and creativity. It wasn't just soccer—it was art. Two European Cups later, he'd not only solidified himself as a player of substance but quietly begun his evolution into a coach of vision.

Calm and composed on the sidelines, he exuded quiet confidence that resonated with his teams. Carlo's tactical brilliance transformed struggling squads into title contenders and nowhere was this more evident than at AC Milan, where he introduced the now-iconic "Christmas Tree" formation (4-3-2-1). This system was both structured and fluid, allowing the midfield to dominate possession while giving creative freedom to players like Kaka and Clarence Seedorf, who thrived behind a lone striker. Deep-lying playmaker Andrea Pirlo orchestrated the game with precision, while full-backs provided width and balance. "Carlo gave us a system, but he never took away our creativity," Pirlo later said, a sentiment many of his players shared.

Yet, his genius wasn't confined to systems and formations. Ancelotti's real gift lay in connecting with his players on a deeply human level. He saw beyond the statistics and performance metrics, understanding their pressures, fears and ambitions. "Carlo understands the man before the athlete," said Kaka, who flourished under his guidance. Cristiano Ronaldo praised him as "a coach who makes you want to run through walls for him." Even the notoriously tough Zlatan Ibrahimović called him "calm but commanding, the perfect leader."

One of Carlo's defining traits has always been his adaptability. At Real Madrid, he managed an ensemble of stars, balancing egos and styles to perfection. His tenure culminated in the club's long-awaited La Décima, their 10th Champions League title, an achievement that etched his name into football history. "He trusted us and we trusted him," said Sergio Ramos. "That's why we succeeded."

But Ancelotti's leadership extended beyond the trophies. During tough moments—like rebuilding Bayern Munich's locker room harmony or restoring Everton's competitiveness—Carlo's empathy and patience shone. He created cultures where players felt heard and valued, fostering loyalty and growth. His belief that "a happy player is a better player" shaped his relationships and it showed on the pitch.

Despite his accolades, Carlo remains remarkably humble. Whether leading Europe's biggest clubs or mentoring young talent, he approaches every challenge with quiet confidence. His ability to navigate different cultures, languages and personalities underscores his flexibility and emotional intelligence.

Carlo Ancelotti's legacy isn't just about his record-breaking titles or tactical brilliance. It's about the way he's empowered players to excel, turned teams into families and taught the world that greatness in football—and life—comes from balance, empathy and an unwavering belief in people. As one of his players put it: "Carlo doesn't just teach you to win—he teaches you how to be better."

In women's soccer, Anson Dorrance stands out as a transformative figure. At the University of North Carolina (UNC), he didn't just forge a winning program; he established a dynasty, setting a new standard in women's sports. "We're not just playing soccer," he would say to his players, "We're building something that lasts." Raised in Mumbai, India, amidst diverse cultures due to his father's job as a petroleum engineer, Dorrance was immersed in soccer from an early age. Transitioning from captaining UNC's men's team to coaching, he significantly influenced women's soccer, shaping its future.

When Anson Dorrance took over UNC's women's soccer program in 1979, he faced a fledgling sports landscape in the U.S.

Without a clear path forward, he forged his own, marrying technical skill with character growth. Central to his strategy was the "competitive cauldron," a novel system that assessed players' performances in every practice, thereby promoting accountability and relentless self-improvement.

This approach transformed UNC's training sessions into battlegrounds of intense competition, where every player's rank was earned, not given. Legends were born from this crucible, including Mia Hamm, who credits Dorrance with teaching her to "fight for everything—not just a spot on the team, but to surpass my own limits."

But Anson's brilliance extended outside the lines of strategy and statistics. He focused on building complete players, both on and off the field. Leadership, resilience and integrity were as important as footwork and passing drills. Team meetings frequently began with discussions about responsibility—owning mistakes, holding oneself accountable and contributing to the team's collective success. "Accountability is non-negotiable," Anson would say. "If you can't hold yourself accountable, you'll never rise to your full potential." Players were encouraged to discuss their struggles openly, whether on the field or off, fostering an atmosphere of trust and camaraderie. "He didn't just prepare us for games," said Kristine Lilly, another star alum. "He prepared us for life."

These meetings often included reflective exercises. Players were asked to write about a moment when they overcame a personal obstacle or share how they planned to contribute to the team's success. Dorrance believed this kind of introspection was crucial. "If you can't understand your own journey," he said, "you can't be the best version of yourself for your team."

Under his leadership, UNC won an unprecedented 22 NCAA women's soccer championships, a record unlikely to be matched. His teams weren't just technically sound—they were relentless, embodying the grit and mental toughness Anson instilled. His influence stretched far beyond the university, shaping stars like Hamm, Lilly and Tobin Heath, who became cornerstones of the U.S. Women's National Team.

Anson's methods weren't without controversy. His relentless drive and brutally honest feedback pushed players to their limits, but those who embraced his philosophy emerged stronger. "He never sugarcoated anything," Heath recalled. "But it made us better—it made us unstoppable."

Off the field, Anson championed women's soccer as a whole, advocating for better opportunities, resources and visibility for the sport. His passion for mentorship extended beyond his players, inspiring countless coaches to adopt his principles of accountability and growth.

Anson Dorrance's legacy isn't just measured in championships or All-American athletes—it's reflected in the leaders, pioneers and changemakers his program has produced. His blend of fierce competition, compassion and unwavering discipline set a standard that elevates soccer, proving that true greatness lies in empowering others to achieve their best. "Soccer is just the beginning," Anson once said. "The real goal is to help these women find the greatness within themselves."

Carlo Ancelotti and Anson Dorrance embody the essence of holistic coaching, acknowledging that an athlete's journey involves more than just skill development. Ancelotti, celebrated for his Champions League victories, fosters trust and resilience, empowering players to take charge of their growth. Conversely, Dorrance, with his NCAA championship wins, prioritizes character and leadership, essential for athletes to succeed both on and off the field. Though applied in different sports, their coaching philosophies share a common goal: to nurture well-rounded individuals equipped to tackle life's challenges. Ancelotti's adaptability and empathetic approach, alongside Dorrance's focus on accountability and competitive excellence, have shaped their sports and offer valuable life lessons on integrity, flexibility and the true meaning of success.

INNOVATION VS. CONSISTENCY: BILL BOWERMAN AND JOHN MCDONNELL

In the realm of track and field, two coaches stand out for their transformative impact on the sport: Bill Bowerman and John McDonnell. Their legacies are defined not just by their achievements but by their distinct philosophies that have left lasting impressions. Bill Bowerman, an iconic coach and innovator in athletics, made his mark with a spirit of restlessness and innovation shaped by his upbringing in the serene hills of Portland, Oregon. As the son of a politician and a teacher, he was driven by curiosity and a constant quest for improvement, often musing, "Why settle for what is when you can create something better?"

Bowerman's drive for excellence transformed the University of Oregon into a track and field powerhouse. Embracing novel methods and individualized coaching, he championed the idea that "Every runner is an experiment of one," customizing training to leverage each athlete's unique capabilities. This approach led to 24 NCAA titles under his guidance and firmly established Bowerman's lasting impact on the sport.

One of his most famous protégés, Steve Prefontaine, embodied Bowerman's philosophy of grit and individuality. A fiery and fearless middle-distance runner, Prefontaine once said, "Bowerman didn't just teach us to run—he taught us how to believe in ourselves." Bowerman pushed Prefontaine to channel his raw talent into disciplined training and encouraged him to question conventional limits. Their bond reflected Bowerman's ability to mentor athletes physically and mentally, fostering a mindset of adaptability and creativity.

Bowerman's most famous innovation didn't happen on the track but in the most unlikely of places—his own kitchen. One morning in 1971, he sat at the breakfast table, staring at his wife's waffle iron, its grid-like grooves catching his eye. For weeks, Bowerman had been toying with different ideas to create a lighter, more flexible running shoe, frustrated by the stiff, clunky designs that slowed his athletes. Suddenly, inspiration struck. Bowerman poured rubber into the waffle iron, letting the mixture harden into a prototype sole.

"I was tired of heavy shoes holding my runners back," he later said. "I thought, 'Why not take something ordinary and make it extraordinary?'" The result was revolutionary—a lightweight, waffle-soled design that provided better traction and flexibility without adding bulk. It was a breakthrough not just in footwear but in how athletes approached performance, shifting the focus to speed and efficiency.

That modest experiment in his kitchen would become the foundation of Nike, the global brand he co-founded with his former athlete, Phil Knight. The waffle sole became iconic, symbolizing Bowerman's inventive spirit and commitment to pushing athletic performance's boundaries.

Yet, Bowerman's vision extended beyond elite competition. In the early 1960s, he stumbled upon the jogging movement during a trip to New Zealand and became an early advocate for running as a form of health and wellness. He co-authored the book *Jogging*, sparking a national fitness revolution that turned running from a niche sport into a cultural phenomenon. Bowerman believed running wasn't just for champions—it was for everyone. "If you have a body, you're an athlete," he famously said, a philosophy that became central to Nike's identity.

Despite his groundbreaking innovations and countless accolades, Bowerman remained humble and focused on the bigger picture. He was never satisfied with winning races or creating products; his mission was to empower others to think differently and push their boundaries. "The real race is against yourself," he told his athletes. And it's the only one that matters."

Bowerman's legacy is a story of transformation—of athletes, sports and the culture around fitness. Through his coaching, inventiveness and passion for helping others, he redefined what was possible in running and left an indelible mark on the world.

John McDonnell's coaching philosophy, rooted in consistency, discipline and meticulous preparation, propelled the University of Arkansas's track and cross-country teams from modest beginnings to a powerhouse, securing an unmatched 40 NCAA national championships. His upbringing on a small farm in County Mayo, Ireland, instilled in him a belief that hard work and daily dedication are the cornerstones of success. This principle guided his journey to Arkansas, where despite limited resources, he proved that resilience and commitment could triumph over any obstacle.

From day one, McDonnell prioritized building a culture of stability and trust. His practices were methodical, focusing on gradual growth rather than quick results. "It's not about how fast you are today," he would tell his athletes. It's about how fast you'll be when it matters most." His training plans blended physical rigor with mental resilience, tailoring regimens to individual strengths while emphasizing long-term goals.

But McDonnell's magic went beyond training. His emphasis on teamwork set Arkansas apart. He cultivated an atmosphere of loyalty and accountability, where athletes ran for themselves and each other. "A true champion isn't just the one who crosses the line first," McDonnell often said. "It's the one who lifts up their teammates along the way." This mindset transformed Arkansas into a tightly-knit family capable of outperforming larger programs with greater resources.

One iconic moment came during the 1984 NCAA Indoor Championships, a pivotal event for McDonnell's Arkansas program. Entering as underdogs, the Razorbacks faced powerhouse teams with greater resources, but McDonnell's squad was prepared. Every athlete played their part: a distance runner surged late to secure second place, a sprinter fought for a critical podium finish and a long jumper hit a personal best when it mattered most. It wasn't about individual glory—it was a collective effort executed with precision and heart.

When the final points were tallied, Arkansas stood as champions, stunning the favored teams. McDonnell rallied his team, declaring, "This is what we do—we win together. Every one of you made this possible." This victory marked the dawn of an era of dominance for Arkansas, establishing the Razorbacks as a collegiate sports dynasty under McDonnell's leadership.

McDonnell demanded integrity and discipline. His athletes knew that excellence on the track was only part of the equation— character mattered just as much. He insisted they carry themselves with pride and responsibility, knowing they represented more than just themselves. "You're not just running for a medal," he told them. "You're running for this team, this school and the legacy we're building."

This approach created champions and leaders. Former athletes often credited McDonnell with shaping their lives beyond sports. "He didn't just teach us how to run," one said. He taught us how to live with purpose."

Focusing on stability, loyalty and gradual growth, McDonnell achieved success that few could match. His ability to create a foundation of trust and unity turned Arkansas into a dynasty year after year. "Sustainability is the true mark of greatness," McDonnell often said and his legacy is proof of that truth.

Today, McDonnell's philosophy remains a blueprint for success in sports and life. He showed the world that greatness isn't built on flashy moments but on hard work, unwavering values and the unbreakable bonds of a team.

Bill Bowerman and John McDonnell are emblematic of track and field's transformative power, each through their unique coaching philosophies. Bowerman, a pioneer, changed the sport with his inventive gear and creative training, urging athletes to push limits and innovate. On the other hand, McDonnell achieved unmatched success at the University of Arkansas with a foundation of consistency, discipline and thorough preparation, creating teams known for their unity and resilience. Bowerman motivated athletes to embrace change and innovation, whereas McDonnell's methodical approach ensured steady progress and peak performance in high-stakes moments. Together, they illustrate that achieving coaching excellence—and success in broader life—requires flexibility, perseverance and a deep investment in developing potential, affirming the variability in pathways to greatness.

INTERCONNECTING THE STORIES OF THE POSITIVE INFLUENCES OF THE SIX COACHES

Exploring the narratives of these exceptional coaches across different sports reveals a unifying theme: their remarkable abilities to take great athletes to the next level. Phil Jackson's Zen-like calm, Pat Summitt's fierce discipline, Carlo Ancelotti's flexible tactics, Anson Dorrance's competitive ethos, Bill Bowerman's creative innovations and John McDonnell's consistent approach—all contribute uniquely to shaping champions and individuals of deep character. They embody the essence of mentorship, emphasizing that true coaching transcends game victories to foster personal growth, teamwork and the pursuit of shared objectives. Envision a serene basketball court under Phil Jackson's guidance, where mindfulness and collective strategy reign. Nearby is a soccer field where Pat Summitt strictly enforces the non-negotiables of hard work and accountability. Both scenarios underscore a commitment to unity and excellence. Similarly, Carlo Ancelotti's adaptability in recognizing each player's unique strengths parallels Anson Dorrance's dedication to character development, proving that personal and skill growth are equally paramount. Bill Bowerman and John McDonnell represent the wide spectrum of coaching philosophies—innovation versus consistency—illustrating that success in coaching, as in life, can be achieved through multiple creative avenues. These stories weave a powerful and compelling narrative that spotlights the transformative power of great mentorship.

———

REFLECTION: FINDING INSPIRATION FROM GREAT MENTORS

Coaches and mentors are often the unsung heroes behind an athlete's success. Their guidance shapes not just careers but character. Whether you're drawn to Jackson's mindfulness, Summitt's discipline, Ancelotti's flexibility, Dorrance's focus on integrity, Bowerman's innovation or McDonnell's steadiness, a good coach's philosophy frequently provides lessons that transcend sports, resonating in the broader challenges of life. These six demonstrate how different coaching philosophies can empower us to achieve our fullest potential. Reflect on these questions to uncover how mentorship might influence your journey:

• *The Mentor in Your Life:* Think about a teacher, coach, family member or friend who has mentored you. What qualities made their guidance impactful? How did they help you grow or overcome challenges?

• *Your Personal Coaching Style:* If you were mentoring someone, what kind of coach would you be? Would you emulate Phil Jackson's calm and mindful approach, Pat Summitt's disciplined leadership or Carlo Ancelotti's flexibility? How does your personality influence the way you guide others?

• *Learning from Different Styles:* Bill Bowerman's creativity and John McDonnell's consistency represent two very different paths to success. Which resonates more with you? Are you more comfortable with structured approaches or do you thrive in an innovative, ever-changing environment?

• *Teamwork and Integrity:* Anson Dorrance emphasized character and teamwork alongside performance. Reflect on a time when teamwork led to a personal or group success. What role did integrity and shared goals play in that outcome?

Take a moment to write down your thoughts. Reflecting on these questions will help you identify the mentorship qualities you value most and how they align with your goals.

ACTION PLAN: EMBRACING MENTORSHIP IN YOUR LIFE

• *Seek a Mentor:* Identify someone who inspires you, such as a teacher, coach or community leader. Reach out to them, share your goals and ask for their guidance. Mentorship is about building a relationship of trust and growth, just as these coaches did with their athletes.

• *Be a Mentor:* Think of someone in your life who could benefit from your experience or encouragement—a younger sibling, a teammate or a friend. Offer to help them with a skill, lend an ear or simply be their cheerleader. You don't need to be an expert to make a difference.

• *Adopt a Coaching Philosophy:* Choose one of the coaching styles from this chapter that resonates with you. Practice applying it in your daily life. For example:

  ◦ Try Phil Jackson's mindfulness by staying calm under pressure and encouraging collaboration in group settings.

○ Emulate Pat Summitt's discipline by holding yourself and others accountable for hard work and focus.

○ Practice Carlo Ancelotti's adaptability by recognizing the unique strengths of those around you and adjusting your approach to bring out their best.

• *Set a Team Goal:* Gather a group of friends, classmates or teammates and set a shared goal. The goal could be anything from winning a game to organizing a school event. Apply this chapter's lessons of teamwork, integrity and shared objectives to achieve it together.

• *Foster Innovation or Consistency:* Reflect on whether you'd like to focus on innovation or consistency in an area of your life, such as school, sports or a hobby. For example:

○ If you value innovation like Bill Bowerman, brainstorm creative solutions for a current challenge.

○ If consistency like John McDonnell's inspires you, commit to a daily or weekly practice that will help you improve steadily.

• *Reflect on Your Progress:* Keep a section of your journal for your experiences with mentorship—both giving and receiving. Write about what you're learning, how it's shaping you and how you're using those lessons to grow. As for other topics, your journal becomes a powerful reminder and playbook for your journey.

• *Celebrate the Wins:* Great coaches celebrate small victories along the way. Whether it's helping someone else succeed, achieving a goal or learning something new, take time to acknowledge and appreciate your progress.

Final thought: The ripple effect of mentorship. We see that mentorship isn't just about winning games—it's about shaping lives. Whether you're seeking a mentor, acting as one or simply applying the lessons you've learned, the influence you create has a ripple effect that can inspire others for years to come. Embrace the power of mentorship and let it guide you toward growth, team-work and achieving your fullest potential.

8 OVERCOMING SOCIAL OR PEER PRESSURE

THE POWER AND PRICE OF SILENT PROTEST: COLIN KAEPERNICK AND TOMMIE SMITH AND JOHN CARLOS

IMAGINE STANDING in front of thousands of fans, the crowd's roar reverberating in your ears and choosing not to speak but to act—to let silence become your voice. This is the essence of protest, a powerful tool wielded by athletes like Colin Kaepernick, Tommie Smith and John Carlos, who have demonstrated that some of the loudest statements are made through quiet, deliberate defiance. Their actions remind us that sports are not separate from society but deeply intertwined with the struggles and triumphs of the human experience.

On August 26, 2016, during the national anthem at a preseason football game, San Francisco 49ers quarterback Colin Kaepernick made his silent statement by sitting alone on the bench. This act, underpinned by his refusal to "stand up to show pride in a flag for a country that oppresses black people and people of color," sparked widespread dialogue on sports activism. Kaepernick's protest, a deliberate choice after months of witnessing systemic injustice, evolved into kneeling during the national anthem after discussions with his friend Nate Boyer, a former Green Beret and NFL player. This gesture of humility and resolve became a symbol of the fight against racial inequality, igniting a nationwide conversation on the role of athletes in social justice movements.

The following game, Kaepernick knelt during the anthem, his head bowed in quiet defiance. This time, the world noticed. The simple act of kneeling sent shockwaves through the sports world and beyond. For some, it was a brave and overdue stand against systemic racism. For others, it was an unforgivable act of disrespect to the flag, the military and the country.

The backlash was immediate. Critics accused Kaepernick of being unpatriotic and politicizing sports, while supporters admired his bravery for highlighting issues larger than the game. Despite the controversy, Kaepernick stood firm, aware of the consequences but committed to giving a voice to the voiceless.

Kaepernick's actions inspired a wave of activism across the sports world. Players from high school teams to professional leagues began kneeling during the anthem, creating what became known as "the Kaepernick Effect." Entire teams locked arms in solidarity, while others refused to take the field until after the anthem. "He gave us permission to speak up," said one NFL player. "He showed us that silence can be powerful."

The movement reignited conversations about the role of athletes in social justice, harkening back to figures like Bill Russell, who stood against racism both on and off the court during his NBA career or Althea Gibson, who broke racial barriers in tennis while facing immense prejudice. Like them, Kaepernick faced immense consequences for his stance, standing firm in his belief that athletes have the power—and responsibility—to challenge injustice.

At the end of the 2016 season, no NFL team signed him, despite his evident talent and history as a Super Bowl-caliber quarterback. It became apparent that his activism had rendered him too polarizing for team owners. Kaepernick, however, refused to waver. "I lost my job," he said, "but I gained my purpose."

His kneeling gesture transcended football, becoming a global symbol of resistance. In 2018, Nike made him the face of their "Dream Crazy" campaign, cementing his status as a cultural icon. The tagline read: "Believe in something. Even if it means sacrificing everything."

Kaepernick's quiet act of protest changed the conversation, forcing a nation to confront its contradictions. His legacy is more than the games he played or the stats he accrued—it's a testament to the power of conviction. He showed that even the simplest gestures, rooted in courage and principle, can ripple across society, inspiring movements and demanding change. Sometimes, the loudest statement is made in silence.

Decades before Colin Kaepernick took a knee, Tommie Smith and John Carlos delivered one of the most iconic and controversial acts of protest in sports history. It was October 16, 1968, at the Olympic Games in Mexico City, a moment charged with tension, courage and an unflinching demand for justice.

Smith and Carlos had already made headlines with their athletic feats. In the 200-meter final, Smith shattered the world record with a blistering time of 19.83 seconds, claiming gold, while Carlos powered his way to bronze. But the real race was just beginning.

In preparation for their iconic protest, Smith donned black gloves and Carlos wore black socks without shoes, symbolizing poverty. Both affixed Olympic Project for Human Rights badges to their attire, committing to a demonstration that would extend their fight for racial equality beyond the track. "We can't just run and leave it at that," Smith told Carlos. "We have to show the world what we stand for."

As they walked toward the podium, the tension was palpable. The stadium buzzed with anticipation yet the men moved with quiet determination. When the U.S. national anthem began to play, Smith and Carlos bowed their heads and raised their fists—gloved in black—toward the sky. It was a stark, defiant image: a call for human rights and a protest against systemic oppression.

The reaction was immediate and explosive. Some in the crowd cheered, but many others booed loudly, outraged by what they saw as a political statement intruding on the apolitical sanctity of the Olympics. The International Olympic Committee (IOC), led by Avery Brundage, condemned their actions as a breach of the Games' rules and demanded that Smith and Carlos be expelled from the Olympic Village.

"We knew it would cost us," Carlos later said, reflecting on that day. "But we felt it was something we had to do—for all the people who had no voice."

The consequences came swiftly. Smith and Carlos were stripped of their Olympic credentials and forced to leave Mexico City. Back in the United States, they faced public backlash and death threats. Sponsors dropped them and their careers suffered. Carlos described being shunned by the same country he had represented on the world stage: "I went from hero to villain overnight."

Yet, Smith and Carlos stood by their actions even as their lives were upended. "I raised my hand for those without rights," Smith explained. "I raised my hand for the voiceless." Their silent protest had spotlighted racial injustice and became a rallying cry for the civil rights movement.

Years later, their act of defiance would be celebrated as a defining moment in the intersection of sports and social justice. It became clear that their bravery extended far beyond athletics. "It wasn't about me," Carlos said. "It was about humanity."

The image of Smith and Carlos on the medal stand, fists raised and heads bowed, remains one of history's most powerful symbols of resistance. Their actions transcended the track, challenging the world to confront uncomfortable truths about inequality and injustice.

Smith and Carlos' protest in Mexico City proved that sports are never separate from society. They showed that an athlete's platform is as much about courage and conviction as it is about competition.

Kaepernick, Smith and Carlos demonstrated extraordinary courage in their statements for racial justice, enduring significant personal and professional sacrifices. Though met with mixed reactions, their silent protests spotlighted the power of leveraging influence to confront societal wrongs. Smith and Carlos faced immediate institutional backlash in the 1960s, while Kaepernick's actions reignited modern debates on patriotism and racial equity. Despite differing contexts, their protests left an enduring mark on the dialogue around social justice in sports and beyond. Their stories underscore that standing for justice often comes at a cost, yet silent acts of defiance can spark profound change. They used their platforms to amplify the voices of the marginalized, embodying true courage by confronting injustice and inspiring movements for equity.

REDEFINING GENDER ROLES IN SPORTS: THE COURAGE OF VENUS WILLIAMS AND JACKIE JOYNER-KERSEE

On the public tennis courts of her neighborhood in Compton, California, a young Venus Williams developed her game. Her racket sliced through the air as she unleashed a powerful serve that seemed to defy her years. Surrounded by chain-link fences and cracked asphalt, Venus and her sister Serena trained with their father, Richard Williams, who was armed with a vision and relentless determination. "We're not just playing tennis," he would say. We're changing the game."

"I just focused on what I could control—my game," she later said. By the time she turned professional at 17, Venus was already a force to be reckoned with, her speed, strength and towering presence setting her apart.

Her breakthrough came in 2000 when she stormed through the Wimbledon draw to claim her first Grand Slam title. With her signature power and unyielding determination, Venus lifted the trophy and announced a new era in women's tennis. "This isn't just my victory," she told reporters, her voice steady. "It's for anyone who's ever been told they don't belong."

Wimbledon became Venus's second home, a stage where she shone brightest. Between 2000 and 2008, she claimed five titles on its hallowed grass, securing her status as one of the sport's all-time greats. Her rivalry with Serena often captivated the world, producing matches that were as much about love and respect as they were about competition. But together, as doubles partners, the Williams sisters were unstoppable, claiming 14 Grand Slam titles and multiple Olympic gold medals.

Behind the scenes, Venus's journey was marked by never giving in. The grueling demands of professional tennis took a toll on her body, leading to injuries that would sideline many players for good. But Venus always returned, defying expectations and continuing to compete at the highest level. "Every time I step on the court, I prove to myself that I can still fight," she said after a hard-fought match in her thirties.

Off the court, Venus Williams became a vocal advocate for gender equality, challenging the glaring issue of unequal prize money in tennis. Grand Slam tournaments had long paid male champions more than their female counterparts, a discrepancy Venus saw as both unfair and demeaning. In 2005, she penned a powerful editorial in The Times, asserting, "The message was clear: Women's work is less valuable than men's."

Venus didn't stop with those words. She met with Wimbledon officials, leveraging her status as a champion to push for change. Her arguments weren't just about money—they were about respect for women's contributions to the sport. "This isn't about me," she told them. "It's about all the players who came before me and those who will come after." Her advocacy gained momentum, drawing support from the WTA, British Prime Minister Tony Blair and other influential voices.

In 2007, Wimbledon's landmark decision to offer equal prize money to men and women was a victory Venus Williams fought hard for. Celebrating it as "a historic day for equality," Venus underscored the achievement's wider implications for gender equity across all fields. This pivotal moment, driven by Venus's advocacy, not only pushed forward the gender equity dialogue but also inspired countless athletes to pursue excellence on their terms. "Venus made us believe we could achieve greatness on our own terms," a young admirer noted, capturing the essence of her impact.

In East St. Louis, Illinois, Jackie Joyner-Kersee raced toward her ambitions amidst scarcity and challenge. Raised in a struggling community, she understood that achieving success demanded more than talent—it required perseverance. "I had to work for everything," she would recall, a testament to her unyielding determination. Sports offered refuge and a platform for her athleticism and resolve to shine. Guided by her grandmother's wisdom and driven by an internal mantra to push beyond fatigue, Jackie excelled in track, basketball and volleyball, setting the stage for her storied athletic career.

Jackie was already making history by the time she competed in the 1984 Los Angeles Olympics. She claimed a silver medal in the heptathlon, narrowly missing gold due to a knee injury. But even in defeat, Jackie's potential was undeniable. "This is just the beginning," she promised herself, vowing to return stronger.

Her defining moment came at the 1988 Seoul Olympics, where Jackie fortified her status as one of the greatest athletes in history. She competed again in the heptathlon, one of the most grueling events in track and field. Spanning two days, the heptathlon tests athletes across seven disciplines, demanding not just versatility but also extraordinary mental and physical endurance. Athletes compete in the 100-meter hurdles, high jump, shot put and 200-meter sprint on the first day, followed by the long jump, javelin throw and 800-meter run on the second. Each event requires a unique blend of speed, strength, skill and strategy and points are awarded based on performance in each discipline.

Jackie's performance in Seoul was legendary. She excelled across all seven events, showcasing her ability to transition seamlessly between the explosive power required in the hurdles and the finesse of the high jump. Her long jump—a personal strength—earned her crucial points, while her grit in the 800 meters, one of the heptathlon's most punishing events, sealed her victory. By the end, Jackie had won the gold medal and shattered the world record with a score of 7,291 points, a mark that still stands today..

She didn't stop there. She returned for the long jump, an event where her explosive power and technique shone once again, earning her a second gold medal. With this dual victory, Jackie Joyner-Kersee became a global icon. "I wanted to show the world that with hard work, anything is possible," she said afterward.

Jackie's path to greatness was marred by persistent injuries that challenged her physically and mentally. Despite battling hamstring and knee problems that threatened to derail her career before the 1992 Barcelona Olympics, her determination prevailed. She clinched gold in the heptathlon and bronze in the long jump, embodying her belief that "Pain is temporary, but giving up lasts forever."

Beyond her athletic achievements, Jackie Joyner-Kersee made a significant impact through her philanthropic work. She established the Jackie Joyner-Kersee Foundation to empower underprivileged youth through education, leadership and health initiatives. "Winning medals was just one part; making a difference was my true goal," she remarked. Her foundation has inspired numerous young individuals to overcome challenges and strive for their dreams.

Jackie's influence reached beyond her community, making her a beacon for gender equality in sports. She openly addressed the hurdles female athletes face, leveraging her stature to champion change. Her journey from adversity to excellence became an emblem of resilience, inspiring both athletes and non-athletes. "Every step, every jump, every throw—it's not just for me," Jackie asserted. It's for all who believe in overcoming."

Both Venus and Jackie have redefined gender roles in sports, each in their own way. Venus's fight for equal pay and her dominance on the tennis court have opened doors for female athletes seeking equality. Jackie's success in track and field has shattered stereotypes about what women can achieve in athletics. Their journeys teach us the importance of steadfastness to a goal, advocacy and breaking barriers.

RISING AGAINST INSTITUTIONAL INJUSTICE: KAREEM ABDUL-JABBAR AND CURT FLOOD

Standing at an imposing 7'2", Kareem Abdul-Jabbar, an NBA legend, was a force of nature. On the court, his skyhook shot was a thing of quiet devastation. It wasn't flashy or theatrical, but it was unstoppable, honed through years of meticulous practice. "I wasn't interested in being flashy," Kareem once said. "I wanted to be effective." And effective he was. Over a 20-year NBA career, Kareem dominated the league, winning six NBA championships, earning six MVP awards and appearing in 19 All-Star games. For decades, he held the title of the NBA's all-time leading scorer, a testament to his consistency, discipline and unparalleled skill.

But Kareem's story wasn't just about basketball—it was about transformation, identity and using his platform to make a difference.

Born Lew Alcindor in Harlem, New York, he grew up in a world of challenges and contradictions. As a young black man in 1950s America, he witnessed both systemic injustice and the resilience of his community. Basketball became an outlet, a sanctuary where his height and talent could shine. He dominated high school basketball at Power Memorial Academy, leading his team to an astonishing 71-game winning streak.

Under legendary coach John Wooden at UCLA, Kareem became a college basketball phenomenon, leading the Bruins to three consecutive NCAA championships. Despite his dominance on the court, he faced intense scrutiny, often being reduced to his physicality rather than celebrated for his intellect and skill. "People saw my height," he reflected, "but they didn't always see the person."

In 1971, after years of introspection, Kareem made a life-changing decision. He converted to Islam and adopted the name Kareem Abdul-Jabbar, a powerful statement of reclaiming his identity and honoring his heritage. "It was about more than faith," he said. It was about self-respect and breaking free from expectations." Some criticized his decision, labeling him ungrateful or un-American. But Kareem stood firm, inspiring others to embrace their identities and challenge societal constraints.

Kareem's commitment to justice and equality became evident early in his career. In 1967, while still in college, he joined the historic Cleveland Summit, where prominent black athletes like Jim Brown and Bill Russell publicly supported Muhammad Ali's refusal to fight in the Vietnam War. Kareem's participation as the youngest member of the group signaled his willingness to stand for his beliefs, even at great personal risk. "I couldn't just dribble a ball and stay silent," he said. "The world was bigger than basketball."

Throughout his NBA career and beyond, Kareem Abdul-Jabbar harnessed his platform to combat racial injustice, educational disparities and police brutality, facing potential backlash with quiet resolve. His post-retirement years saw him evolve into a prolific writer and cultural ambassador, passionately discussing systemic racism and the transformative power of education in works such as *Giant Steps* and *Writings on the Wall*. As a compelling speaker, he urged audiences towards uncomfortable yet necessary conversations about equality, encapsulating his assertion, "We can't afford to be silent. The fight for justice is one we all share."

From his dominance on the basketball court to his relentless pursuit of justice, Kareem Abdul-Jabbar's legacy is one of transformation—of himself, of sports and society. His story reminds us that greatness isn't measured in points or championships but in the courage to stand for something bigger. "Being a champion," he once said, "isn't just about what you achieve—it's about what you give back."

Curt Flood wasn't the loudest name in baseball, but his presence was undeniable on the field. He was poetry in motion in center field for the St. Louis Cardinals—gliding effortlessly to make impossible catches. Flood earned seven Gold Gloves, batted consistently over .300 in several seasons and played pivotal roles in the Cardinals' World Series championships in 1964 and 1967. But while his talent shone on the diamond, his courage off the field made him a true pioneer.

In 1969, Flood was traded to the Philadelphia Phillies and he faced a pivotal moment. Unlike most players who felt powerless against baseball's reserve clause, Flood took a stand. "I had given my all to the Cardinals," he declared, refusing to be seen as mere property. His resistance, articulated in a bold letter to MLB Commissioner Bowie Kuhn, challenged the league's foundational practices. This defiance set the stage for a landmark legal battle, pressing for players' rights and freedom within the sport.

In 1970, Flood filed a lawsuit against MLB, claiming that the reserve clause—which bound players to their teams indefinitely—violated antitrust laws and basic freedoms. The case Flood v. Kuhn became a landmark in sports history. Flood knew the odds were stacked against him. Baseball had operated under the reserve clause for nearly a century and owners had little interest in relinquishing control.

The legal battle was grueling and Flood faced immense backlash. Fans called him ungrateful; team owners blackballed him. Even some fellow players distanced themselves, fearful of jeopardizing their own careers. "It was a lonely fight," Flood admitted years later. "But it was the right fight."

The case reached the Supreme Court in 1972. Flood's lawyer, Arthur Goldberg, argued passionately that the reserve clause was an unjust system that treated athletes as commodities rather than individuals. Despite the compelling case, the court ruled against Flood in a 5-3 decision, citing baseball's long-standing exemption from antitrust laws.

Flood may have lost the legal battle but his stand lit a fire that couldn't be extinguished. His courage inspired a movement among players, and just a few years later, the reserve clause crumbled. In 1975, thanks to the work of Marvin Miller and the MLB Players Association, free agency became a reality, forever altering the dynamics of professional sports.

The cost of Flood's defiance was immense. After his stand, his baseball career was effectively over, as no team would sign him. Financial struggles and emotional strain followed and Flood himself admitted the toll was heavy. Yet, his sacrifice paved the way for generations of athletes to have control over their careers.

Flood's impact extended far beyond the ballpark. His fight resonated as a broader stand against injustice and inequality. He became a symbol of what it means to challenge entrenched systems, even when the odds seem insurmountable. "Curt Flood was my hero," said Hall of Famer Reggie Jackson. "Without him, none of us would have had the freedom we do now."

Today, every time an athlete signs a lucrative free-agent contract or chooses their own path, they stand on the shoulders of Curt Flood. "I didn't do it for myself," Flood said in a rare interview late in life. "I did it because it was the right thing to do—for every player who comes after me." Curt Flood was a baseball player, a revolutionary, a man who dared to change the game not just for himself but for everyone.

Flood and Kareem Abdul-Jabbar emerged as pivotal figures who confronted institutional injustices through their platforms. Abdul-Jabbar championed racial equality while Flood fought against the constraints of restrictive contracts, advocating for athlete autonomy. Both faced significant professional and personal risks, yet their actions catalyzed crucial reforms in sports, showcasing the transformative power of standing up against injustice. Their legacy illustrates that meaningful change often begins with the courage of a single step, underscoring the impact of using one's voice to challenge the status quo.

INTERCONNECTING THE STORIES OF OVERCOMING SOCIAL AND PEER PRESSURE OF THESE SEVEN ATHLETES

Facing a crowd that once applauded them, now casting ridicule because they dared defy norms—this was the reality for athletes like Colin Kaepernick and Kareem Abdul-Jabbar. Each faced immense pressure to conform, enduring public criticism, professional backlash and personal sacrifice. Their careers and legacies were at risk, yet they remained solid in their beliefs. Colin Kaepernick's silent protest and Venus Williams's fight for equal pay reveal the isolation often faced when standing up for justice while showcasing the power of purposeful commitment and the lasting imprint of bravery. Along with Tommie Smith, John Carlos, Jackie Joyner-Kersee and Curt Flood, they defied societal norms and transformed the conversation, forcing a discussion of uncomfortable realities. The stories of these athletes weave together the threads of staying true to one's core beliefs, bravery in the face of criticism and steadfast determination, illustrating how standing firm against unfairness can inspire real change and influence generations.

As you reflect on these stories, consider the giant lessons they teach. Each athlete faced moments of doubt, where the easier path might have been to remain silent or conform. Yet, they chose to speak out, risking their careers and reputations for the greater good. Their actions show us that integrity, guts and self-belief are not just values to aspire to but are the necessary tools for making change. Their stories encourage you to think critically about your own choices and the paths you wish to take.

———

REFLECTION: WHAT DO YOU STAND FOR?

The athletes in this chapter remind us that staying true to our beliefs, even when it's hard (especially when it's hard), is one of the most courageous acts we can undertake. Their stories of resilience in the face of immense social and peer pressure highlight the power of conviction and integrity. Reflect on these questions to explore your own relationship with pressure and personal values:

• *Core Beliefs:* Think about an issue or cause you feel strongly about. Why does it matter to you? How far would you be willing to go to stand up for it, even if others disagreed or judged you?

• *Handling Criticism:* Colin Kaepernick and Venus Williams faced intense backlash for their choices. Have you ever experienced criticism or pressure to conform? How did it feel and how did you respond? What did you learn from the experience?

• *Solidarity and Support:* Kareem Abdul-Jabbar and Tommie Smith found strength in solidarity with like-minded people. Who in your life supports your beliefs and values? How can you build a network that empowers you to stay true to yourself?

• *Defining Your Legacy:* Curt Flood's stand for fairness reshaped sports, even at great personal cost. What kind of legacy do you want to leave behind? How can your actions today align with the values you want to be remembered for?

Take some time to write down your thoughts. Reflecting on these questions will help you clarify your beliefs and how you might navigate the pressures you face.

ACTION PLAN: BUILDING THE COURAGE TO STAND UP FOR YOUR VALUES

• *Identify Your Values:* Write down three values that are most important to you (e.g., fairness, honesty, kindness, equality). Keep this list somewhere you can see it, like your journal or phone, as a reminder of what guides your decisions.

• *Practice Speaking Up:* Start small by speaking up in situations where you see something wrong. This might mean standing up for a friend, voicing your opinion in a group or addressing a small injustice in your community. Practice builds confidence.

• *Build Your Support Network:* Identify people who share your values or who will stand by you when things get tough. Reach out to them, share your goals and discuss how you can support one another in staying true to your beliefs.

• *Learn from Role Models:* Choose an athlete from this chapter whose story resonates with you. Research more about their journey, the pressures they faced and how they overcame them. Write down one or two lessons from their experience that you can apply to your life.

• *Prepare for Resistance:* Think about situations in which you might be pressured to conform or remain silent. Practice how you might respond, such as calmly explaining your stance, walking away or seeking support from others.

• *Channel Your Convictions into Action:* Choose a cause you care about—whether it's equality, mental health, environmental protection or another issue—and find a way to contribute. It could be volunteering, starting a conversation or joining a school or community group.

• *Stay True to Yourself:* When faced with peer or social pressure, take a moment to pause and ask yourself: Does this align with my values? Would I feel proud of this choice later? Use your reflections as a guide to stay authentic.

• *Inspire Others:* Just as these athletes inspire change, your actions can motivate those around you. Share your story, encourage others to stand up for what they believe in and celebrate acts of courage and integrity within your community.

Final thought: Your voice, your power. The athletes in this chapter demonstrate that standing firm in the face of pressure isn't only about individual courage—it's about sparking change and inspiring others. Whether you're confronting a personal challenge or advocating for a larger cause, your voice and actions have the power to make a difference.

Start small, stay committed and remember that every choice you make to stand up for what you believe in strengthens not only your character but also the world around you. Take that step when your conscience tells you it's necessary—you never know who you might inspire along the way.

TWO MINUTE WARNING

As we reach the end of our journey through "Game Changers: Inspirational Sports Stories," take a moment to reflect on some of the incredible tales of perseverance, leadership and resilience we've encountered. At the heart of this book is the understanding that sports offer more than just competition; they're a transformative force that teaches valuable life lessons. Whether it's overcoming adversity, embracing cultural identity or leading with courage, the athletes you've read about have shown that greatness is achieved through dedication and heart.

The multiple-narrative approach offered us a fun and distinctive way to share these fascinating stories. By weaving together the journeys of different athletes or coaches under a unifying theme and exploring their similarities and differences, we observed how different experiences can teach similar life lessons. This approach allowed us to compare contrasting paths, offering a deeper and more nuanced understanding of the values discussed. It has reinforced for us that, despite diverse journeys, the foundational principles of perseverance, courage and leadership are universally relevant.

Several key takeaways have emerged from these stories. You've learned about the power of self-discovery and how understanding yourself can be a game-changer. Embracing cultural identity stands out as a theme, showcasing how being true to oneself can lead to empowerment. The importance of mentorship resonates throughout, emphasizing how guidance from others can shape your journey. Additionally, the significance of mental toughness and the courage to challenge social norms reveal that strength must also come from within.

Life is a varsity sport. Now that you've moved from the practice squad to a starting spot, it's your turn to continue reflecting. Think about the challenges you face and the values you've seen described in this book. How can you apply these lessons to your own life? Consider your personal experiences and how the stories of these athletes might inspire new ways of overcoming obstacles. Remember, the qualities that make these athletes exceptional are not beyond your reach.

Let's translate these insights into action. Set personal goals that push you toward growth. Seek out mentors who can guide you on your path. Embrace diversity and learn from those around you. Engage in community service or team activities to build resilience and character. These steps can help you develop skills and confidence, molding you into a well-rounded individual and an emerging leader.

Your journey doesn't end here. Use the inspiration from these stories to fuel your continued growth. Sports can be a lifelong source of learning and empowerment. Keep exploring your passions and striving for excellence in all areas of your life. The lessons from this book are tools for navigating challenges and seizing opportunities.

As you look back on these stories of athletes from various backgrounds, celebrate their uniqueness. Each athlete brought something special to the table and you can do the same. Value your individuality and recognize the unique contributions you can make to your community and beyond.

I want to leave you with an uplifting and accurate message: the potential for greatness lies within you.

You have the power to be a "Game Changer" in your own life. Use the examples of these athletes to guide you in discovering and deepening your core values. Use the lessons from this book to crush your personal goals. Use them to inspire others and create positive change in the world. Remember, it's not just about the victories on the field but also about the impact you make off it.

Thank you for taking this journey together. I hope these stories have sparked something within you and encouraged you to pursue your dreams with determination and courage. Keep pushing forward and never forget that you have the power to change the game.

You got this.

FINAL WHISTLE

Thank You for Reading Game Changers: Inspirational Sports Stories.

I hope these stories have resonated with you and offered meaningful insights into resilience, character and the transformative power of sports.

If this book has inspired you, I kindly ask one more time: if you haven't already, please consider sharing your thoughts by leaving a review on Amazon. Your feedback can make a meaningful difference, helping others discover these stories and the lessons they hold.

Reviews don't need to be long or detailed—a quick rating and a few words about how the book impacted you are enough. For **e-book readers**, simply click the link below to be taken to the Amazon review page. For those with the **printed version**, scan the QR code with your phone's camera to access the same page.

Your review has the power to inspire others, encourage them to explore their potential and remind them of the strength within. By sharing your experience, you're becoming part of the book's mission to uplift and empower other young people.

Thank you again for being a part of this journey. Together, let's continue inspiring others to become Game Changers in their own lives.

Review link coming soon.

QR code coming soon.

Keep an eye out for the next book in the series, "Game Changers 2: Inspirational Coaches' Stories." Coming soon!

ABOUT THE AUTHOR

Dan Gold is a father, friend, forever learner and Fairfield, CT resident. Growing up in the midwest, his experiences shaped a strong passion for both sports and storytelling. After exploring a couple of professions and learning some valuable life lessons along the way, he has reached the "I'd better write it down" stage in life. Dan's writing explores themes of self-discovery, resilience, love, relationships and how to lead a more meaningful life. As an author, Dan is focused on creating books that inspire young readers to build confidence, cultivate character, form meaningful connections and aim high.

BIBLIOGRAPHY

- SPYSCAPE. (n.d.). *Serena Williams: From sports star to tennis superhero.* Retrieved from https://spyscape.com/article/serena-williams-from-sports-star-to-tennis-superhero#:~:text=Growing%20up%20as%20a%20black,talent%20and%20determination%20silenced%20critics

- Moneycontrol. (2023). *Messi was diagnosed with a growth disorder when he was 11—How he overcame it.* Retrieved from https://www.moneycontrol.com/news/trends/messi-was-diagnosed-with-a-growth-disorder-when-he-was-11-how-he-overcame-it-9729001.html

- Axon, R. (2024). *How Simone Biles moved mental health discussion forward. USA Today.* Retrieved from https://www.usatoday.com/story/sports/olympics/2024/07/19/simone-biles-mental-health-gymnastics/74454444007/

- Understood.org. (n.d.). *Celebrity spotlight: How Michael Phelps' ADHD helped him make Olympic history.* Retrieved from https://www.understood.org/en/articles/celebrity-spotlight-how-michael-phelps-adhd-helped-him-make-olympic-history#:~:text=Phelps%20was%20diagnosed%20with%20ADHD,famed%20swim%20coach%20Bob%20Bowman

- Hamilton, B. (n.d.). *Bethany's story.* Retrieved from https://bethanyhamilton.com/biography

- Triathlete. (n.d.). *The science and controversy of running blade prosthetics.* Retrieved from https://www.triathlete.com/culture/the-science-and-controversy-of-running-blade-prosthetics/

- International Tennis Hall of Fame. (n.d.). *Andre Agassi.* Retrieved from https://www.tennisfame.com/hall-of-famers/inductees/andre-agassi#:~:text=Agassi%20walked%20away%20from%20the,3%2C%206%2D4

- Belson, K. (2024, November 14). *Lindsey Vonn will end her retirement and rejoin the U.S. ski team. The New York Times.* Retrieved from https://www.nytimes.com/2024/11/14/us/lindsey-vonn-world-cup-retirement.html

- Llopis, G. (2018, May 29). *4 transformational things LeBron James teaches us about leadership and teamwork. Forbes.* Retrieved from https://www.forbes.com/sites/glennllopis/2018/05/29/4-transformational-things-lebron-james-teaches-us-about-leadership-and-teamwork/

- Global Citizen. (n.d.). *Soccer star Abby Wambach is fighting to close the gender wage gap.* Retrieved from https://www.globalcitizen.org/en/content/abby-wambach-she-is-equal-gender-wage-gap/

- Golub, J. (2018, November 27). *The difference between quiet leadership and no leadership*. *The Stanford Daily*. Retrieved from https://stanforddaily.com/2018/11/27/golub-the-difference-between-quiet-leadership-and-no-leadership/#:~:text=Kawhi%20Leonard%20is%20an%20introvert,for%20his%20commitment%20and%20discipline
- The Irish Times. (2020). *Steffi Graf was the pioneer of a new age in women's tennis*. Retrieved from https://www.irishtimes.com/sport/other-sports/steffi-graf-was-the-pioneer-of-a-new-age-in-women-s-tennis-1.4291472
- USA Basketball. (2015, November). *How Michael Jordan's mindset made him a great competitor*. Retrieved from https://www.usab.com/news/2015/11/how-michael-jordans-mindset-made-him-a-great-competitor
- Imagery Coaching. (n.d.). *Martina Navratilova's mental game*. Retrieved from https://www.imagerycoaching.com/the-edge-blog/martina-navratilovas-mental-game
- Tennis World USA. (2020). *Novak Djokovic on how he learned to overcome self-doubt on the court*. Retrieved from https://www.tennisworldusa.org/tennis/news/Novak_Djokovic/87223/novak-djokovic-on-how-he-learnt-to-overcome-self-doubt-on-the-court/
- Essence. (n.d.). *Allyson Felix reflects on her mental health during Olympic trials*. Retrieved from https://www.essence.com/entertainment/allyson-felix-reflects-on-her-mental-health-during-olympic-trial-season/
- University of Louisville Library. (n.d.). *Muhammad Ali: Social justice and civil rights icon*. Retrieved from https://library.louisville.edu/ali/SocialJustice_CivilRights
- AS USA. (n.d.). *Megan Rapinoe's social activism: LGBTQ+ rights, racial justice, and pay equity*. Retrieved from https://en.as.com/soccer/megan-rapinoes-social-activism-lgbtq-rights-racial-justice-pay-equity-n/
- Complex. (n.d.). *Anthony Joshua on the importance of community*. Retrieved from https://www.complex.com/sports/a/jacob-davey/interview-anthony-joshua-community-crime-wilder
- NBC Washington. (2023). *How former Georgetown coach John Thompson Jr. saved Allen Iverson's life*. Retrieved from https://www.nbcwashington.com/news/sports/nbcsports/how-former-georgetown-coach-john-thompson-jr-saved-allen-iversons-life/2406194/
- MLS Multiplex. (2023). *Hope Solo: A controversial and remarkable journey in women's soccer*. Retrieved from https://mlsmultiplex.com/2023/08/05/hope-solo-a-controversial-and-remarkable-journey-in-womens-soccer/
- E! Online. (2017). *How Alex Rodriguez went from doping scandals to taking over sports television*. Retrieved from https://www.eonline.com/news/870913/how-

alex-rodriguez-went-from-doping-scandals-to-taking-over-sports-television-and-dating-jennifer-lopez-you-have-to-own-your-s-t

- ESPN. (n.d.). *Exclusive: Marion Jones talks about 'Life After.'* Retrieved from https://www.espn.com/blog/playbook/trending/post/_/id/10836/exclusive-marion-jones-talks-about-life-after

- CRM. (n.d.). *Zen and the art of winning: Phil Jackson's team leadership.* Retrieved from https://crm.org/articles/zen-and-the-art-of-winning-phil-jack sons-team-leadership

- NCAA. (2016). *Pat Summitt: Read the legendary coach's 'Definite Dozen' rules.* Retrieved from https://www.ncaa.com/news/basketball-women/article/2016-06-28/pat-summitt-read-legendary-coachs-definite-dozen-rules

- Leaders in Sport. (n.d.). *What makes Carlo Ancelotti one of the most successful leaders in European football.* Retrieved from https://leadersinsport.com/perfor mance-institute/articles/what-makes-carlo-ancelotti-one-of-the-most-success ful-leaders-in-european-football/

- The Fayetteville Observer. (2024). *Anson Dorrance channeled Dean Smith, developed a competitive cauldron.* Retrieved from https://www.fayobserver.com/story/sports/college/acc/2024/08/12/anson-dorrance-unc-women-soccer-dean-smith-competitive-cauldron-tar-heels-coaching/74381870007/#:~:text=The%20competitive%20cauldron%20is%20de-signed,They%20are%20ranked

- Princeton University. (n.d.). *The Kaepernick effect: How a knee inspired a generational revolt.* Retrieved from https://aas.princeton.edu/news/kaepernick-effect-how-knee-inspired-generational-revolt#:~:text=By%20%E2%80%9Ctak-ing%20a%20knee%2C%E2%80%9D,to%20America%27s%20persistent%20ra-cial%20inequality

- History.com. (n.d.). *Why Black American athletes raised their fists at the 1968 Olympics.* Retrieved from https://www.history.com/news/black-athletes-raise-fists-1968-olympics

- WTA. (2024). *Venus Williams recalls fight for equal pay.* Retrieved from https://www.wtatennis.com/news/3677769/you-cant-beat-the-truth-venus-williams-recalls-fight-for-equal-pay#:~:text=It%20was%20a%20t-wo%2Dyear,equal%20prize%20money%20in%202007

- ESPN. (2023). *Kareem Abdul-Jabbar's lifetime as a social justice champion.* Retrieved from https://www.espn.com/nba/story/_/id/35602384/kareem-abdul-jabbar-life-social-justice-champion-record-no-athlete-break#:~:text=In%20the%20public%20record%2C%20Ka-reem,was%20the%20youngest%20person%20there

Printed in Great Britain
by Amazon

58612081R00096